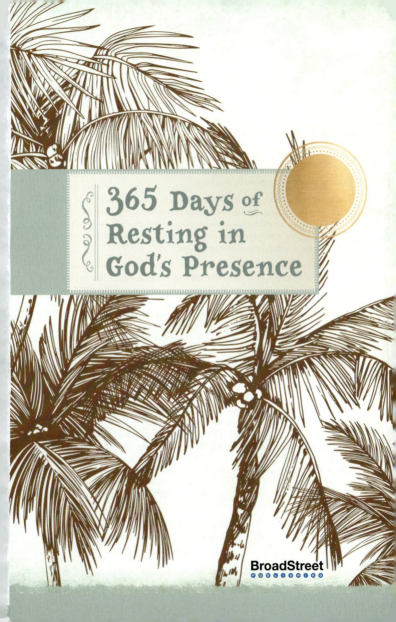

BroadStreet Publishing Group, LLC.
Savage, Minnesota, USA
Broadstreetpublishing.com

365 Days of Resting in God's Presence
© 2025 by BroadStreet Publishing®

9781424570195
9781424570201 (eBook)

Devotional entries composed by Sara Perry.

All rights reserved. No part of this publication may be reproduced, distributed, or transmitted in any form or by any means, including photocopying, recording, or other electronic or mechanical methods, without the prior written permission of the publisher, except in the case of brief quotations embodied in critical reviews and certain other noncommercial uses permitted by copyright law.

Scripture quotations marked NIV are taken from the Holy Bible, New International Version®, NIV®. Copyright © 1973, 1978, 1984, 2011 by Biblica, Inc.™ Used by permission of Zondervan. All rights reserved worldwide. www.zondervan.com. The "NIV" and "New International Version" are trademarks registered in the United States Patent and Trademark Office by Biblica, Inc.™ Scripture quotations marked NLT are taken from the Holy Bible, New Living Translation, copyright ©1996, 2004, 2015 by Tyndale House Foundation. Used by permission of Tyndale House Publishers, Carol Stream, Illinois 60188. All rights reserved. Scripture quotations marked ESV are taken from the ESV® Bible (The Holy Bible, English Standard Version®), Copyright © 2001 by Crossway, a publishing ministry of Good News Publishers. Used by permission. All rights reserved. Scripture quotations marked CSB are taken from the Christian Standard Bible®, Copyright © 2017 by Holman Bible Publishers. Used by permission. Christian Standard Bible® and CSB® are federally registered trademarks of Holman Bible Publishers. Scripture quotations marked NASB are taken from the New American Standard Bible, Copyright 2020 by The Lockman Foundation. Used by permission. All rights reserved. Scripture quotations marked NKJV are taken from the New King James Version®. Copyright © 1982 by Thomas Nelson. Used by permission. All rights reserved. Scripture quotations marked NCV are taken from the New Century Version®. Copyright © 2005 by Thomas Nelson. Used by permission. All rights reserved. Scripture quotations marked TPT are taken from The Passion Translation® of the Holy Bible. Copyright © 2020 by Passion & Fire Ministries, Inc. Used by permission of BroadStreet Publishing®. All rights reserved.

Typesetting and design by Garborg Design Works | garborgdesign.com
Editorial services by Michelle Winger | literallyprecise.com and Natasha Marcellus.

Printed in China.

25 26 27 28 29 30 31   7 6 5 4 3 2 1

Introduction

In the hustle and bustle of life, finding a moment of true rest can seem impossible, but God invites you to step into his presence and experience the profound peace that only he can provide. This devotional is your guide to embracing his invitation each and every day.

With thoughtful reflections, carefully selected Scriptures, and heartfelt prayers, *365 Days of Resting in God's Presence* will help you draw closer to God's heart. Rest in his goodness as his promises are illuminated. Connect deeply with him as you express your innermost thoughts and desires.

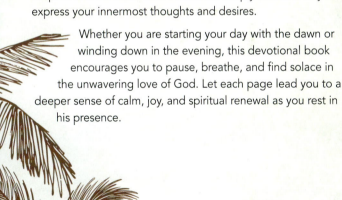

Whether you are starting your day with the dawn or winding down in the evening, this devotional book encourages you to pause, breathe, and find solace in the unwavering love of God. Let each page lead you to a deeper sense of calm, joy, and spiritual renewal as you rest in his presence.

January

Truly my soul finds rest in God;
my salvation comes from him.

PSALM 62:1 NIV

JANUARY 1

This Is the Day

*This is the day the LORD has made.
We will rejoice and be glad in it.*

PSALM 118:24 NLT

A lot of people like to look toward the future at the beginning of the year. Today may be the start of a new calendar year, but it is also an opportunity to be rooted in the present. Each and every day is a gift. None of us know how long we will be on this earth, so it's to our benefit to embrace each day with intention, gratitude, and joy.

God is present with you in this very moment. He doesn't wait for special moments to show up. He is as close in this breath as he ever was or will be. Turn your attention to his nearness. Thank him for the gift this day offers. Find reasons to rejoice here and now, and rest in the presence of God's love as it washes over you. There is no better time than the present to lean into the goodness of God.

Good God, thank you for this day. Thank you for life, connection, and all you have given. I choose to rest knowing you are near. I rejoice in the present because it's full of your love.

JANUARY 2

Seasons and Cycles

> There is a time for everything,
> and a season for every activity under the heavens:
> a time to be born and a time to die,
> a time to plant and a time to uproot.
>
> ECCLESIASTES 3:1-2 NIV

There is a season for everything. There is a time to press in, and a time to pull back. There is time to work, and time to rest. Knowing which season we are in can help us arrange our priorities. When we fight the reality of our circumstances, we miss the chance to rest in God's goodness despite the details of our days.

It would be foolish to have a summer wardrobe at the ready in the height of the cold winter months. It would be much wiser to keep warmer clothes accessible. When you engage with your surroundings realistically, you set yourself up for success. When your expectations are reasonable, you remain ready for whatever comes your way. Take time to look over the current season of your life and ask the Lord to show you how to embrace it.

Holy Spirit, thank you for the wisdom of the seasons. I don't want to fight the winters of life. Help me embrace the season you have me in right now. I don't want to wish away your plans for my life.

JANUARY 3

Power of Purpose

*He made the moon to mark the seasons;
the sun knows its time for setting.*

PSALM 104:19 ESV

The moon and sun were created with purpose. There is power in their very existence. Where would we be without the sun? Would the earth be what it is without the moon to shift tides and seasons? If the sun and moon reflect God's intentions in their existence, we can be sure that we do too.

There is purpose in your life, and you don't have to create it. You were born to bloom as a child of God. You were knit together with specific talents and giftings. Your purpose is built into your existence. The sun and moon don't determine when to shine or when to shift the seasons. They are already fulfilling their purposes. Rest in your identity as a beloved child of God. Lean back into the steady arms of your Savior and let him bless you with his presence.

Creator, I don't want to strive for my worth. I want to rest in who you have created me to be and live fully and freely in the light of your love.

Lay Them Down

"Come to me, all of you who are tired and have heavy loads, and I will give you rest."

Matthew 11:28 NCV

When the heavy burdens of life weigh us down, we don't have to buckle under their load. Jesus invites us to come to him with everything we carry. He beckons us to lay our burdens at his feet and experience real rest in his presence.

In prayer, turn your attention to Jesus and release what you carry. He will take your worries and give you peace. It's a beautiful exchange. He is strong enough to help you, and he is eager to relieve you. He longs for you to trust him and take him up on his offer of peace.

Faithful One, I bring you all the burdens, worries, and confusion I carry. I trust you to give me rest and peace when I surrender to you.

JANUARY 5

Safe and Secure

*Because of you, Lord, I will lie down in peace
and sleep comes at once,
for no matter what happens, I will live unafraid!*

Psalm 4:8 tpt

There are times in life when sleep becomes elusive. We struggle to rest when we can't stop thinking about the troubles around us. We dwell on what's going on in the world, in the lives of those we love, and in our own backyards. However, this is not how God wants us to live. He wants to soothe our worries just as a caring parent does for their child.

If you are having trouble sleeping, consider changing your bedtime habits. Instead of looking at your phone, try reading. When you feel yourself begin to ruminate, turn your attention toward your day. What are three things for which you are grateful? Look for where his light shines through the cracks of your life. You can lie down in peace and sleep unafraid because God watches over you.

Good Father, I trust you to take care of what I cannot. When the troubles of this life are many, open my eyes to see the way you've blessed me. Please soothe my heart and give me peaceful sleep.

Present Peace

"My presence will go with you, and I will give you rest."
Exodus 33:14 CSB

It is okay if you have struggled to recognize God's presence. It does not change his faithful nature one bit, and he doesn't grow tired of assuring you of his love. If you need a fresh reminder of his grace, ask him for it. If you need courage to step forward, remember that his presence goes with you.

The peace of God isn't fragile. It does not recede with your confusion or frustration. The Lord is powerfully present no matter the situation or circumstance. It doesn't matter what time of day or night it is. If you need him, you can be sure that he is accessible. Open your heart to him and watch as he meets you in the midst of whatever you are experiencing.

Prince of Peace, I confess that I need your peace again. I need reassurance of your presence once more. Thank you for your patience and compassion toward me. Settle my heart and mind as I turn to you.

JANUARY 7

Ancient Paths

*"Stand by the ways and see and ask for the ancient paths,
Where the good way is, and walk in it;
Then you will find a resting place for your souls."*

JEREMIAH 6:16 NASB

God has laid out a path for each of us. We can faithfully follow him because he is trustworthy and good. He will order our steps and keep us steady. He will lead us by the hand when we can't tell which way to go. The path of faith has been walked by many before, and we can trust that the way is well marked.

When you walk in God's ways, you will find rest. Though the terrain might be unknown or difficult, he will give you exactly what you need. The rest you experience in your soul far surpasses any amount of physical rest. The confidence that comes from knowing you are following a reliable leader is better than anxiously stumbling through life without him. Today, stretch out your hand and trust God to guide you.

Lord, you have set a path before me. Give me strength to walk in your ways and follow you with confidence. I trust you to give me exactly what I need along the way.

JANUARY 8

Sabbath Rest

There remains therefore a rest for the people of God. For he who has entered His rest has himself also ceased from his works as God did from His.

HEBREWS 4:9-10 NKJV

In the beginning, God created the world. He created the mountains and seas, along with everything in them. He set the stars and planets in motion. He made animals and plants alike, and he also created humanity. When he was finished, he didn't simply move on. He didn't keep fine-tuning it, either. He stepped back and admired everything he made, and he said it was good. Finally, he rested.

You don't need permission to rest; you already have it. You were made for it, and it's important to take time to step away from your work and responsibilities. If you don't already have a set Sabbath, make room in your schedule. Even if you cannot set aside a whole day, you can piece together times of rest. Create rhythms of rest in your schedule, and you will be grateful you did.

God, thank you for the example you have set. Help me follow you by making time to rest. I want to know the joy, peace, refreshment, and restoration of keeping a Sabbath.

JANUARY 9

Feast on Joy

> Taste and see that the LORD is good.
> Oh, the joys of those who take refuge in him!
>
> PSALM 34:8 NLT

Joy is not reserved for easy times. It isn't available only when everything seems to be going right in the world. Joy is found in the presence of God. He is always good, and we can celebrate his goodness no matter the time or season.

Take time to look for the goodness of God in your life. He has given you so many good gifts. From the peace of a quiet morning to the laughter of a loved one, life is filled with reasons to give thanks to God. As you taste and see his goodness, remember how much he loves you. As you find your home in him, rejoice and be glad!

God, I don't ever want to forget how good you are. Open my eyes and fill my heart with overflowing gratitude as I look for the fingerprints of your mercy in my life.

JANUARY 10

Return and Rest

This is what the Sovereign Lord, the Holy One of Israel, says:
"In repentance and rest is your salvation,
in quietness and trust is your strength."

Isaiah 30:15 NIV

Repentance is an uncommon word, but it is not complicated. It is a change of heart and mind that brings us closer to God. It involves embracing humility and asking forgiveness, but it also involves turning away from sin and toward God. When we repent, we reorient our heart and deliberately surrender our will to God's.

There is rest in returning to the Lord. There is peace that settles over your heart as you receive his forgiveness and know the freedom of his grace. Whatever distance you have felt from the Lord, he closes the divide as soon as you turn to him. Don't be afraid to go to him, no matter how long or short it's been since you last connected with him. He is always ready to receive you. Return and rest, beloved child of God.

Merciful Father, thank you for the peace I find in you. You are my soul's home, and I find my rest in you.

JANUARY 11

Soul Satisfaction

"I will satisfy the weary soul, and every languishing soul I will replenish."

JEREMIAH 31:25 ESV

We cannot avoid weariness in this life. Inevitably there will be days and seasons that feel harder than others. When we find ourselves in these times, let's not use our weariness as a weapon against ourselves. God gives strength to the weak. He is close to the brokenhearted. He draws near to the humble of heart.

When your soul is languishing, don't despair. God offers grace, compassion, and the strength of his love. It can be tempting to feel worthless when you are in a dormant period in life and aren't experiencing the progress or thriving you had hoped. However, your worth is not tied to what you do! It is in who God says you are, and that never changes. May your soul find its satisfaction in God today and every day.

Shepherd of my soul, I find it hard not to find my worth in what I can offer. Help me to know the power and peace of your love as it meets me as I am today.

JANUARY 12

Sustained

> I can lie down and go to sleep,
> and I will wake up again,
> because the LORD gives me strength.
>
> PSALM 3:5 NCV

Whether you are starting the day fresh or reflecting at its end, may today's verse fill your heart with peace. You can lie down and sleep, and you will wake again because the Lord gives you strength. He is your sustenance, your source, and your help. You are not alone, and you never will be.

God's faithfulness continues from day to day and age to age. He hasn't missed a moment of your life. His well of mercy will never run dry. God meets you in the mundane and the extraordinary, in the horrible and in the overwhelmingly good. Breathe in his peace and remember his nearness. God is your source of sustenance and strength.

Powerful One, I'm so thankful for your faithfulness and unchanging nature. You are always merciful, good, gracious, and kind. You are my strength and my soul rests in you.

JANUARY 13

Confident Trust

Perfect, absolute peace surrounds those whose imaginations are consumed with you; they confidently trust in you.

Isaiah 26:3 TPT

The imagination is a wonderful gift. It is not only for our entertainment, dreaming, or leisure. It is where our mindsets are shifted, our hope is bolstered, and our faith is expanded. God is not offended by our imaginings of him. He loves to meet us in the place of creative ideation!

You cannot exaggerate the goodness of God. Your fullest understanding is barely a glimpse of his glorious reality. Scripture says that God will outdo our greatest requests and exceed our wildest imaginations. Instead of praying small, stretch your imagination and expect the goodness of God to meet you in powerful ways. Rest in the absolute peace of God's powerful love today.

Glorious God, there is no one like you. I quickly forget how powerful and loving you are, but you never change. Overwhelm my expectations with the reality of your goodness!

JANUARY 14

Abounding Hope

May the God of hope fill you with all joy and peace as you believe so that you may overflow with hope by the power of the Holy Spirit.

ROMANS 15:13 CSB

Sometimes hope feels scarce. Our attitudes and faith are tested daily, but there is good news. God is as faithful today as he was when he led his people through the Red Sea on dry land. He is as loving and kind as he was when Jesus ministered to the poor, healed the sick, and raised the dead. He hasn't changed one bit.

When your hope is in God, you have a never-ending source to draw from. When you feel despair creeping in, it's time to redirect your attention. Be aware of what is draining your energy. While it is good to stay informed about the world, you are not built for constant information overload. Be sure to give your nervous system, mind, and our heart a break to rest in the presence of God. The Holy Spirit offers you peace, joy, and hope as you rest in him.

God of hope, help me find my rest, joy, and peace in your presence. Give my body, mind, and soul a break from the noise of endless information.

JANUARY 15

Lie Down and Rest

He lets me lie down in green pastures;
He leads me beside quiet waters.
He restores my soul;
He guides me in the paths of righteousness
For the sake of His name.

PSALM 23:2-3 NASB

Psalm 23 evokes powerfully peaceful imagery. The Lord is a good shepherd. He doesn't overwork his sheep. He leads us beside quiet waters so that we will know the restoration of his peace. He allows us to lie down in green pastures so that we can experience the rest and provision that only comes from him.

Picture a quiet body of water. Imagine the way the sun might shine and the noises of nature you might hear. Perhaps there is a hammock close by where you can nap. This is the kind of rest your soul can find in God today. He is gentle with you, and he knows exactly what you need. Spend time with him and ask him to lead you to the place of rest where his peace washes over you.

Good Shepherd, lead me beside quiet waters and restore my soul. Thank you for the green pastures of your presence. Fill me with peace as I trust you to lead me.

JANUARY 16

Plentiful Portion

> My flesh and my heart fail;
> But God is the strength of my heart and my portion forever.
>
> PSALM 73:26 NKJV

God's power is not contingent upon our strength. No matter what state we are in, he is powerful, merciful, faithful, and true. In this world, we admire the vitality of youth. We put our value in what we can offer, or how we appear to others. This is not the way of God's kingdom. His opinion of us does not change depending on our age. He is with us fully for all of our days.

When your heart and flesh fail, embrace your weakness. There is vulnerability in authenticity. Put aside the need to look a certain way and instead go to God with your frailty. He knows you through and through. He is your plentiful portion. When you are at your weakest, he has all the strength you need.

God, I don't want to pretend with you. You see me as I am with all my flaws and weaknesses. Strengthen my heart with your gracious love.

JANUARY 17

Powerful Peace

Then you will experience God's peace, which exceeds anything we can understand. His peace will guard your hearts and minds as you live in Christ Jesus.

PHILIPPIANS 4:7 NLT

There is no fear in God's love. He offers us peace so we can be considerate, grounded, and wise. When we offer our hearts to him, he offers us the blessings that come from living according to His design. This means choosing peace over chaos, joy over fear, and trust over anxiety.

God's peace allows space for you to be confident and grounded even when your circumstances could merit fear or frustration. His peace doesn't shut you down or overlook your feelings. Instead, it allows you to securely stand upon the truth no matter how you feel. God's peace is steady, reliable, and unshakeable.

Gracious God, your peace is incredible. It calms nervous systems and storms alike. When fear threatens to cause chaos in my life, bring me back to your presence and fill me with peace.

JANUARY 18

Focus on His Face

> Look to the LORD and his strength;
> seek his face always.
>
> 1 CHRONICLES 16:11 NIV

In the Old Testament, the face of God was synonymous with his presence. When we seek his face, we seek his presence. Each day we can center ourselves and turn our attention toward God. He is always close and ready to be found. We don't have to journey to the ends of the earth to find him.

Look to the Lord no matter where you are or how you're feeling. Expect his strength to meet you in your weakness. Seek his face always, for it is to your benefit to be intertwined with his heart. He loves to meet you where you are, empower you in your weakness, and refresh your hope when you need it.

Lord, I look to you today. I let go of the worries that have been clouding my focus and turn my attention to you, the author and perfecter of my faith. Meet me here, Lord. I need you.

JANUARY 19

God Alone

*For God alone my soul waits in silence;
from him comes my salvation.*

Psalm 62:1 esv

Typically, we don't have many friends who stay by our side for the entirety of our lives. Some friends come and go with the different seasons of life. Others are close in heart but far in distance. Friends are a gift from God, but the greatest gift we have is Jesus. He never leaves us. He never misunderstands us. He is always close.

Jesus is your salvation and provision. Everything you truly need is found in him. He loves you unconditionally and is the wisest of counselors. When you feel alone, remember that He is close and available. He is ready to embrace you with open arms. Wait on him and experience the refreshing rest of his presence once again.

Savior, there is so much in life that I cannot control. When others cannot meet me in my need, you always do. I don't take your presence for granted. Thank you for loving me and providing for me.

JANUARY 20

Body and Soul

My dear friend, I know your soul is doing fine, and I pray that you are doing well in every way and that your health is good.

3 John 1:2 NCV

John's prayer for his friend in today's verse is a good reminder to pray for wholeness in the lives of those we love, as well as in our own lives. God doesn't want us to experience peace in our souls alone; he wants us to know the power of his faithful love in every way including in our bodies.

Where are you doing well? Thank God for these areas. Where do you need God's help in experiencing more balance, rest, and strength? Offer these areas to him. Don't settle for certain areas of your life being good enough. Bring whatever you are lacking to your faithful Father and allow him to decide what is best for you. He cares about every part of you.

Lord, thank you for giving me new life through Jesus. Thank you for the healing and wholeness you continue to bring to my life. Help me turn to you with my weaknesses and trust you with the areas of my life that are lacking.

JANUARY 21

Daily Bread

"I am the Bread of Life. Come every day to me and you will never be hungry. Believe in me and you will never be thirsty."

JOHN 6:35 TPT

The promises of God are yes and amen. They are hope to our souls and strength to our bones. Jesus' ministry powerfully reflected God's heart toward his people. He is the Bread of Life. He quenches the thirst of our souls with the living waters of his love. There is no better place to start our day than in the nourishing presence of Christ our daily bread.

Just as food fuels our bodies for all that we encounter, Jesus gives us all we need to energize our faith and empower our hearts in his love. God gives us what we need each and every day. His Word is never stale, and his presence opens doors to provision. Spend time with him every day, and feast on his timely Word.

God, thank you for your daily bread. Speak to me and encourage my heart in the power of your wisdom. I trust that you will supply all I need today and every day. Thank you.

JANUARY 22

Invitation to Rest

"Come away by yourselves to a remote place and rest for a while." For many people were coming and going, and they did not even have time to eat.

MARK 6:31 CSB

God does not want us to burn out. Jesus knew the importance of getting away from the demands of others. He invited his friends and disciples to retreat with him. They needed respite from the ministry and its demands. If Jesus embraced the importance of rest, then we can do. We can follow his example without guilt.

You aren't meant to work non-stop. You aren't meant to be so overloaded with responsibilities that you can't step away to breathe, re-focus, and find the nourishment you need. Maybe you can't get away for a weekend, but you can likely find a place near you that puts some distance between you and your responsibilities. God has given you permission to step away and allow your soul to be refreshed.

Jesus, thank you for the reminder that rest is necessary. You took time for yourself, so I don't have to feel bad about doing the same. Help me prioritize stepping away from the demands of life and resting so I can come back feeling refreshed.

JANUARY 23

Tower of Strength

> The name of the Lord is a strong tower;
> The righteous runs into it and is safe.
>
> Proverbs 18:10 nasb

God's nature is like a strong and mighty tower. It is a safe place to retreat when we feel overwhelmed by the demands of life. On days when everything seems to go wrong and we can't seem to gain perspective, God is with us. We don't need to be at our best before we come to him. He is a good Father who delights in helping his children.

When the storms of life are out of hand and you need a place to rest, go to the Lord. Even when you can't physically remove yourself from a difficult situation, you can connect to the Lord in your innermost being. You can turn your heart toward him and rest in the quiet peace of his presence. He is your strength, and he will not let you fight your battles alone.

Great God, I'm so thankful for your powerful presence that is accessible at all times. I run to you and find safety, peace, and all that I need.

Let Go and Trust

Anxiety in the heart of man causes depression,
But a good word makes it glad.

Proverbs 12:25 NKJV

Anxiety is not a restful state. When we are hyper vigilant, there isn't space to let go and rest in the present peace of God. While we may not be able to rid ourselves of every worry or anxiety, we can hand them over to the Lord. We can know the peace of his presence as it meets us in every breath.

A good word at the right time brings relief. It breaks through the what-ifs and eases the unknown with powerful truth. You can know the power of God's presence as you turn your attention to his nearness. He is with you, just as he promised he would be. When anxiety rises in your heart, offer it to the Lord and trust him with your stress. Quiet your soul and wait in his presence. He has words of life to offer you.

Father, anxiety is like a leaky faucet that never lets up, but your peace is more powerful. I offer you the worries of my heart and let go of the need to understand every detail of my life. Speak to me and flood me with your peace.

JANUARY 25

Rest for Everyone

"You have six days each week for your ordinary work, but on the seventh day you must stop working. This gives your ox and your donkey a chance to rest. It also allows your slaves and the foreigners living among you to be refreshed."

EXODUS 23:12 NLT

All living beings need a break. It is important that we prioritize rest and also encourage it in the lives of others. Endless hustling doesn't add value to anyone's life. We may be fine for a time, but we cannot avoid resting forever. Eventually we will have to deal with the repercussions of enduring when we should be looking for refreshment.

Don't resist rest. Build it into your schedule. Make time for connections, hobbies, and habits that are life giving. Maybe you've let your schedule get too crowded and can't find time for the things you enjoy. Deliberately adjust your priorities as an act of preemptive care. It isn't selfish to rest. It is important, biblical, and what God wants for you.

Lord, I don't want to be so busy that I never take time to rest. It's so easy to pack my schedule until the margins are used up. Help me prioritize doing things that bring me life and refreshment.

JANUARY 26

Eternal Encouragement

May our Lord Jesus Christ himself and God our Father, who loved us and by his grace gave us eternal encouragement and good hope, encourage your hearts and strengthen you in every good deed and word.

2 THESSALONIANS 2:16-17 NIV

God's truth is powerful, and it will bring life and light to whoever seeks it. He is gentle with us in our weakness, and he is always full of wisdom and compassion. Even his correction is laced with kindness. May we know the encouragement, hope, and strength of God's love as we move throughout our days. Each of us is fully seen, known, and loved.

Are you in need of encouragement today? It is available in the fellowship of God right now. You don't have to button yourself up or hide your messes. He receives you as you are. Bring him the reality of your heart and mind. Lay your life before him and don't hold back. He won't be offended by your honesty.

God, what a wonderful father you are. Thank you for your gentle truth and unwavering love. I trust you with my tender heart. I bring you all I am and invite you to move in my life as you will.

JANUARY 27

Born to Bear Fruit

The fruit of the Spirit is love, joy, peace, patience, kindness, goodness, faithfulness, gentleness, self-control; against such things there is no law.

GALATIANS 5:22-23 ESV

Constant attention doesn't lend itself to a well-producing tree. It is possible to over prune and stunt the tree's growth. On the other hand, neglect doesn't serve a plant's best interest either. Care happens in the combination of helpful intervention and space for the plant to heal and grow. While pruning is necessary, so is time for the plant to thrive afterward.

You can't constantly work on yourself and expect that you will bear more fruit as a result. You need rest, sunshine, and rain. You need periods of weeding and pruning, but you also need time to bloom. Don't overwork yourself. There is beauty in rest, and there is power in allowing yourself to recharge. God made you that way, so don't fight it!

Maker, thank you for the reminder that I don't need to manage my own pruning. Keep me from thinking that I must always be productive. Teach me to embrace every stage from pruning, to rest, to bearing fruit.

JANUARY 28

Supernatural Blessing

He said, "Throw your net on the right side of the boat, and you will find some." So they did, and they caught so many fish they could not pull the net back into the boat.

JOHN 21:6 NCV

In the aftermath of Jesus' death, many of the disciples went back to the only life they knew before they followed him. Simon Peter, unable to make sense of anything, decided to go fishing. His friends went with him. At daybreak the following day, Jesus stood on the shore and asked them if they caught any fish. In response to their negative reply, he instructed them to throw their net over the right side. When they did, there was an incredible abundance.

God graciously meets us in the same way. He offers wisdom, and when we obey, we see the abundance of his power and mercy at work. Let's listen for the voice of our Savior and do as he suggests today. There is abundant blessing awaiting us in obedience. Even when we are discouraged and cannot solve our problems alone, God is with us.

Savior, thank you for the power of your miracles in my life. I will listen for your voice, for you always know what to do.

JANUARY 29

It's Simple

"Simply join your life with mine. Learn my ways and you'll discover that I'm gentle, humble, easy to please. You will find refreshment and rest in me. For all that I require of you will be pleasant and easy to bear."

MATTHEW 11:29-30 TPT

Jesus is gentle, humble, and easy to please. He isn't a taskmaster, and he isn't irritable. Think of the most pleasant person you know. What is it like to be around them? Jesus is even better. He is the refreshment and rest you need. Join your life with his, and you will know the powerful goodness of his nature.

Read today's verse again, this time paying close attention to what stands out to you. There is so much life in the Word of God, and what speaks loudest to you today may be different from what hits you tomorrow. Ask the Spirit to breathe life into the Word as you read and meditate on it.

Savior, you are the best friend I could imagine. You are better than I expected at every turn. Even when I walk through the shadows, your light shines brightly, and you are my comfort. Thank you.

JANUARY 30

Sustenance

"It is written: Man must not live on bread alone but on every word that comes from the mouth of God."

MATTHEW 4:4 CSB

Our bodies need nourishment for survival and for thriving. God wants the same thing for our souls. There is so much goodness in his Word. There is more than sustenance to get us by. He gives us what we need, and he offers abundant blessings that go above and beyond. He gives us all that we need to live a full, whole, healthy life.

You may think you know what is best, but you don't see the full picture. God takes account of factors you don't realize are at work. He works all things together for the good of those who love him, and he guides you with his wisdom. As you follow along the path of surrendered love, you will find there is more than enough to satisfy your soul. His ways are worth following, for his Word is true, and his love is unfailing.

Lord Jesus, you are the embodiment of the Word, and I find nourishment for my heart in your presence. You are my source of hope, and you give me everything I need. Thank you for helping me every step of the way.

JANUARY 31

A Hopeful Future

"'For I know the plans that I have for you,' declares the Lord, 'plans for prosperity and not for disaster, to give you a future and a hope. Then you will call upon Me and come and pray to Me, and I will listen to you. And you will seek Me and find Me when you search for Me with all your heart.'"

JEREMIAH 29:11-13 NASB

God has not lost sight of you. No matter what obstacles you face, he knows the plans he has for you. They are not for your detriment; they are for your growth and your good. When you think about the future, he wants you to be filled with hope. Call upon the name of the Lord, and he will listen. Seek him with your whole heart today, and you will find him.

However you feel about your future today, you can find rest in God's faithfulness. There is no obstacle that intimidates him. There is no challenge that is insurmountable. He will give you a way through every trial you face. Trust him and call on him whenever you need help. He is close, and he is ready to encourage and equip you.

Father, when my heart is heavy, show me the hope I have in you. Open my eyes to see where your light shines so that I may taste and see your goodness every day.

February

He makes me lie down in green pastures,
he leads me beside quiet waters,
he refreshes my soul.

Psalm 23:2-3 niv

FEBRUARY 1

In Your Need

*"The poor and needy seek water, but there is none,
Their tongues fail for thirst.
I, the Lord, will hear them;
I, the God of Israel, will not forsake them."*

Isaiah 41:17 NKJV

God sees your every need. There isn't a problem he is unaware of or a challenge he has missed. He will not forsake you. Scripture says he will not only give you what you need, but he will also give you rest as you wait on his provision. He longs to be involved in every step of your journey. Walk alongside him even when you don't know the next step, and he will faithfully guide you.

When you cannot make movement happen on your own, as this verse alludes to, God will hear you. He will not abandon you. He will make a way where there is none. He made water gush from a rock in the desert to satisfy the thirst of the Israelites, and he can miraculously provide for you as well. Trust him, for he is faithful, loyal, and true.

God, I trust you to provide for me in every season. When I am tired of striving, help me surrender to you. Give me peace as I confidently wait for your faithful provision.

FEBRUARY 2

Be Still

> He calmed the storm to a whisper
> and stilled the waves.
>
> PSALM 107:29 NLT

God's power knows no bounds. He is not limited by the weaknesses we experience in our humanity. He is willing and able to do far more than we can ask or imagine. We can pray big, bold prayers, for he is more powerful than we know. Instead of holding back or playing it safe, we can confidently ask God for whatever we need.

God has calmed more than one storm in history. He quieted waves with his voice, and he can calm the turmoil that rages within you. No heart is so stormy that he cannot bring peace and order to it. If you need God's presence to settle your nerves today, place a hand over your heart and invite him to do what he does best. Ask the Holy Spirit to move within you and receive his peace.

Prince of Peace, calm the chaos within me. Quiet my nerves and replace my worries with peace. Bring order and calmness to the parts of me that need it most.

FEBRUARY 3

Comforted

*I have calmed and quieted myself,
I am like a weaned child with its mother;
like a weaned child I am content.*

PSALM 131:2 NIV

Most of us have known the soothing touch of a caregiver's embrace. There is something powerful about being held in our discomfort and pain. God is a tender Father who holds us close. If he offers us compassion and gentleness, then we should look at ourselves with that same perspective.

You can partner with God by holding space for your own experiences of grief and frustration. Instead of pushing the pain aside, allow it to exist and witness it with loving compassion. As you do, you will learn to find peace in connecting with God instead of suffering on your own. God offers you comfort in his presence, and he longs for you to accept it.

Holy Spirit, I invite your peace to flood my heart even as I experience the reality of pain, disappointment, and grief. When I am hurting, remind me that you are space place to bring my emotions. Thank you for teaching me how to view myself with gentleness and compassion.

FEBRUARY 4

Breathe in Peace

May the Lord of peace himself give you peace at all times in every way. The Lord be with you all.

2 Thessalonians 3:16 ESV

God's peace is like the air, extending farther than we can comprehend and doing more in our systems than we realize. Most of us don't have to think about breathing. We take for granted the oxygen we take in, but it is necessary to life. We may only begin to notice its power when we find ourselves in situations where its quality is compromised.

In the same way, the peace of God is available like pure oxygen to our souls. Our need for it may become more heightened when pollution, smoke, and foul odors invade our senses. Instead of despairing at the presence of chaos, we can experience the life-giving peace of God's presence. His peace is like a fresh, open field of undiluted air. It revives our soul and fills us with new life.

Lord, peace is the atmosphere of your presence. In you, I live, move, and have my being. Remind me of my desperate need for your peace.

FEBRUARY 5

Overflowing Joy

*You will teach me how to live a holy life.
Being with you will fill me with joy;
at your right hand I will find pleasure forever.*

PSALM 16:11 NCV

Joy and pleasure are not afterthoughts in the kingdom of God. They are sown into the very fabric of God's ways. His wisdom leads us to life. His love brings us freedom. His grace offers a light and joyful way. Living a holy life isn't about what we give up; it is about what we gain in God's great mercy.

If you want more joy in your life, get to know Jesus. If you want to know true freedom, it is found in the gracious salvation of Christ. He doesn't put stipulations on his gift of grace, and he doesn't demand perfection from his people. There is no fine print to fool you, and there are no hidden caveats to navigate. He is better than you could ever expect or understand.

God, I have tasted joy, but I am ready for more today. My soul is refreshed in the lavish love of your presence, and you fill me with gladness!

FEBRUARY 6

Wholehearted Trust

> Trust in the Lord completely,
> and do not rely on your own opinions.
> With all your heart rely on him to guide you,
> and he will lead you in every decision you make.
> Become intimate with him in whatever you do,
> and he will lead you wherever you go.
>
> PROVERBS 3:5-6 TPT

We can trust God, not because we have to, but because everything he does comes from a foundation of lovingkindness. There is no shadow of shame, corruption, or malice in his heart. He is gracious, patient, and kind. We don't have to get by on our own knowledge or opinions because the God of infinite wisdom is eager to lead us in truth.

God is always for you. This does not mean you will always get your way or that he withholds correction or guidance. When you rely on him to lead you through the twists and turns of life, he will not remove every obstacle. He will help you around or through them with integrity, grace, and love. If you trust him to guide you, you will not be left wanting.

Lord, I want to know the power of your loving and trustworthy nature more than I ever have. Help me trust you as you guide me step by step today. I rest in your unfailing wisdom and love.

FEBRUARY 7

Sacrificial Love

"For God so loved the world, that He gave His only Son, so that everyone who believes in Him will not perish, but have eternal life."

John 3:16 NASB

God's love is tested and true. It isn't self-seeking or surfacy. He offers it generously to all who will receive it. If we look for his love wholeheartedly, we will not be left disappointed. He revealed his love by sending his Son to redeem us through his death and subsequent resurrection. Jesus' sacrifice means that God's love is available to everyone equally.

There is nothing standing between you and God's great love. Jesus has removed every barrier. If you need a reminder of the power of God's love, you don't need to look any further than the life of Christ. He is God's Word incarnate. He is the love of God on display for all. Jesus is your powerful Savior, and his love reaches you, sets you free, and gives you rest.

Christ Jesus, I want to know the power of your love in fresh ways today. Open my eyes to the limitless mercy of God's heart as I look to you and read the Word.

Necessary Margin

Understand this, my dear brothers and sisters: You must all be quick to listen, slow to speak, and slow to get angry.

JAMES 1:19 NLT

Resting is like gathering resources in anticipation of a storm. We know that conflicts and trials are inevitable, so it makes sense to be prepared for them. People will rub us the wrong way, so it is wise to strengthen our character knowing it will be tested. If we want to be able to listen well, refrain from talking over others, and be slow to anger, it is in our best interest to prioritize times of rest and refreshment.

There will always be more you *can* do at any given time, but that doesn't mean you should. You need stillness as much as you do movement. When you build margins into your life, you create space to rebuild your emotional and physical resources. If you want to genuinely love others, your well must be full. Where can you pencil in time for yourself, as well as time with loved ones who will fill your cup?

Father, I don't want to overlook my need for rest. When I am well rested, I am able to listen better and stay calm. Give me grace to fill my own well so I can love others from a place of strength.

FEBRUARY 9

Door to Rest

"I am the door. If anyone enters by Me, he will be saved, and will go in and out and find pasture."

JOHN 10:9 NKJV

Jesus is the door to salvation, and he is also the door to true rest and freedom. As long as we are on this earth, we will come up against limits to our love, but God does not have any limits. When we come to Christ, he ushers us into the peace of his presence, the confidence of his faithfulness, and the nourishment of his love.

What do you long for today? What does your heart need? Bring it all to Jesus. Walk through the door of his presence and receive everything he has stored up for you. His kingdom is full of abundant peace, generous grace, and powerful mercy. All that you heart longs for is available in the heart of the Father.

Jesus, you are the door to eternal life, but I know you offer me daily blessings as well. I want to receive the rest you offer at this very moment. Fill my heart with peace and help me remember you are my true source of rest.

FEBRUARY 10

Courage for Today

*"Don't be afraid, for I am with you.
Don't be discouraged, for I am your God.
I will strengthen you and help you.
I will hold you up with my victorious right hand."*

ISAIAH 41:10 NLT

God doesn't look at our circumstances and demand our blind allegiance. He doesn't tell us to be courageous with no foundation to stand upon. His promises are sure, and his presence is pervasive. Why should we take courage in the midst of disappointment? Why should we press on in the face of challenges? We can endure those things because God is our ever-present help in times of need.

Has fear caused you to waver, or has discouragement tempted you to quit? There are times to rest and times to press on. It's important to know what is required of you. Ask the Lord to show you the path for today. Maybe courage looks like letting yourself off the hook. Maybe it looks like taking that one step you've been avoiding. Whatever it is, remember God is with you, and he will help you.

Victorious One, your faithful presence and overwhelming love give me courage. I will follow you today even if I feel unsteady. Strengthen me in my weakness and give me grace to stay close to you.

FEBRUARY 11

Flourish

*That person is like a tree planted by streams of water,
which yields its fruit in season
and whose leaf does not wither—
whatever they do prospers.*

Psalm 1:3 niv

When we choose to follow the Lord, walking in his ways and partnering with his loyal love, we remain rooted in his life-giving presence. The fruit of our lives reveal the fruit of his Spirit. Righteousness is found in yielding our lives in surrender to the leadership of God. It is found in fellowship with the King of kings and Lord of lords.

If you want to flourish, make God your delight. Let his fellowship nurture your heart and lead you into alignment with his love. There is no better place for you to grow, rest, and flourish than in a relationship with the Creator of all things. He knows you through and through, and he wants you to know him in the same way. Seeking him will never leave you disappointed.

Lord, the fruit of your love is undeniable. It brings grace, peace, joy, generosity, hope, willpower, and delight to my life. As I know you more, my heart awakens to the life you offer and the abundance of your lavish love.

Take Heart

> "I have said these things to you, that in me you may have peace. In the world you will have tribulation. But take heart; I have overcome the world."
>
> JOHN 16:33 ESV

Jesus didn't shy away from telling his disciples the hard truth of what was to come. He also didn't withhold his encouragement or kindness. God doesn't need our positive spin on reality. He doesn't need us to ignore the hard things of life as we cling to him. He gives us courage to live in the tension of what is and what is to come. His presence is sure, his love is unfailing, and his kingdom is eternal.

Let Jesus be your place of peace today, no matter what is going on in the world. You don't have to deny what is challenging in order to know his peace in the midst of it. He graciously offers you everything you need out of the riches of his kingdom. Trust him and he will give you peace as you surrender.

Lord, you are my foundation and my shelter. I run to hide in you, not to deny what is happening in the world, but to find respite in the midst of it. Thank you for your very present peace. It is my comfort, my strength, and my hope.

FEBRUARY 13

Eyes on Him

*Wait and trust the LORD.
Don't be upset when others get rich
or when someone else's plans succeed.*

PSALM 37:7 NCV

When we measure ourselves based on the success of others, it is easy to fall into the trap of comparison. Though others may succeed in their plans, that doesn't mean anything for our own path. It doesn't take away from what God has for us, and it doesn't mean that we are doing better than anyone else. There is room enough for everyone follow God and cheer each other on in the process.

Envy only steals from your relationships. It robs you of joy, hope, and peace. When you redirect your focus from others to the Lord, you will receive his perspective which is full of love, goodness, and limitless grace. Your journey through life is unique and shouldn't be compared to anyone else. Celebrate when others succeed, even if your victories don't look the way you expect them to.

Lord, align my heart with yours and give me your perspective. Fill me with joy when people around me succeed. When I am tempted to compare my life to others, give me grace to trust in your plans alone.

FEBRUARY 14

Abundant Life

> "A thief has only one thing in mind—he wants to steal, slaughter, and destroy. But I have come to give you everything in abundance, more than you expect—life in its fullness until you overflow!"
>
> JOHN 10:10 TPT

God's heart is full of generosity and goodness. He does not have hidden motives for our destruction. He has open intentions of kindness toward us. As we unabashedly open our hearts to him, he offers us abundant life.

While there are people who seek to steal, kill, and destroy, the people of God stand apart. We reflect the power of his love, offering grace to those who fail us, forgiveness to those who hurt us, and kindness to those who wish us harm. We are builders of life and love. We serve our communities for the common good not for what we get out of it. This is what abundant life looks like and how we can reflect the extravagant love of Christ.

Lord Jesus, thank you for the power of your life-giving kindness that refreshes and restores all who experience it. I choose to live according to your love today. Give me grace to lay my life down however you lead me to.

FEBRUARY 15

The Greatest Standard

"Love the Lord your God with all your heart, all your soul, all your strength, and all your mind." Also, "Love your neighbor as you love yourself."

LUKE 10:27 NCV

Jesus said the whole of the law could be summed up in the standard of love. When we love someone with our whole hearts, we are moved to honor them and maintain a close connection with them. Honor, generosity, and kindness are beautiful reflections of a heart that is full of love.

If you want to walk in the fullness of God, love must be your priority. Love God not only with words, but with actions. Love others by offering grace, kindness, and truth even when you don't feel like it. Let Christ-like love be your intention every day. Relationships matter more than tasks, so be sure that love leads you to connection because that's what it's all about.

God, thank you for the power of your love that sets the captives free, heals the sick, and raises the dead. Show me opportunities to reflect your love to the people around me.

Primary Focus

> "Seek first the kingdom of God and His righteousness, and all these things shall be added to you."
>
> MATTHEW 6:33 NKJV

Every day there are needs to be met, people to connect with, and responsibilities to fulfill. When we spend all our attention on how our needs are met, our hearts may grow weary. We need a greater perspective and vision. Jesus made it clear that when we first seek him and his kingdom, everything else will fall into place.

What has been your primary focus lately? What monopolizes most of attention? What has your emotional energy been spent on? There is so much peace to be found in prioritizing knowing and being known by God. When you spend time with him, he will calm your anxiety and remind you that he is in control. The more you surrender to him, the more room he has to guide you along the right path.

Righteous God, you are my vision. I seek your kingdom and your heart today. Help me trust you with the details of my life. When I wander away from you, pull me back. When I am distracted, give me grace to redirect my focus.

FEBRUARY 17

Defender

The LORD will fight for you, and you must be quiet.

EXODUS 14:14 CSB

Sometimes, there is absolutely nothing we can do to change a situation or someone else's perspective of us. Instead of pushing harder when we face barriers of all kinds, we can allow God to fight for us. He knows the truth, and he knows just what to do on our behalf.

We don't see the full picture, but God always does. He knows exactly what needs to be said and done in every situation to bring peace, clarity, and justice. Every seemingly hopeless situation is an opportunity to rest in God's presence and trust that he will fight for us. He is our defender, and he will not fail.

Defender, thank you for the reminder that I don't have to push harder in the face of opposition. When I have done all I can, I lean back and let you take the lead. I follow your leadership and rest in your wisdom.

Wherever You Go

> "This is my command—be strong and courageous! Do not be afraid or discouraged. For the LORD your God is with you wherever you go."
>
> JOSHUA 1:9 NLT

There is nowhere we can go to escape God's presence. This is such wonderful news! We cannot wander so far away that he cannot reach us. No matter where we are his Spirit is present. There is no place we could hide from him. There is no place where we are stranded without him.

God's pervasive peace is accessible in any and every circumstance. Wherever your feet lead you today, he is there. He is our help. You can be strong and courageous as you rest in his faithfulness. You are never alone, and he is always ready to help. Abide in his presence and he will give you courage to face whatever comes.

Eternal One, thank you for your constant presence. Thank you for being with me even when I don't feel like you are. Give me unwavering confidence that you are always near.

FEBRUARY 19

In Quiet Rest

The fruit of that righteousness will be peace;
its effect will be quietness and confidence forever.

ISAIAH 32:17 NIV

Righteousness produces peace. It is not a promoter of dissension or fear. If our righteousness is in Christ, he is our confidence. He is our source of peace and the one who quiets our soul. He is our holiness, our righteousness, and our redemption. We rest in his finished work and find restoration in his presence.

When you are confronted by your own limitations, turn your attention to God's perfect love. He doesn't expect perfection from you. He wants you to know the power of his peace by resting in his righteousness. Take on the garment of his love and walk in his ways. When you falter, trust that his strength is more than enough for your weakness.

Righteous One, I have spent so much time striving to be better. Help me rest in the powerful sufficiency of your grace. I surrender to you in my weakness. Flood me with peace and give me rest.

FEBRUARY 20

Measureless Grace

*Cast your burden on the L*ORD*,
and he will sustain you;
he will never permit
the righteous to be moved.*

P*SALM* 55:22 ESV

There is no burden too great that the Lord will not take it from you. Offer him your cares and anxieties, leaving them at his feet today. He offers you boundless grace in return. He longs to sustain and strengthen you with his powerful love. Instead of shouldering more responsibility, let go and ask God what you should be carrying.

It is not a virtue to feel personally responsible for everyone around you. It isn't good for your soul to give others compassion and offer none to yourself. The Lord wants you to know the freedom of his grace, and you can only experience it by letting go of what you cannot control. Lean into the faithful love of God and trust him to guide you. He is the one who will provide for you and everyone around you.

Gracious God, I don't want to be burdened by things you never meant for me to bear. I offer you the weight of my worries, and I leave them at your feet. I trust that you are able and willing to lead me every day.

FEBRUARY 21

Incomparable Delight

> I was very worried,
> but you comforted me and made me happy.
>
> PSALM 94:19 NCV

When was the last time you felt the overwhelming delight of relief? Worry weighs us down, but God's comfort brings peace, clarity, and joy. We cannot control what will happen tomorrow, but we can trust the one who can. He is full of love, and his comfort settles and soothes our busy minds.

God knows how to bring calm to your chaos. Trust him to do it today and every day. The relief of knowing that he is in control can be enough to settle your heart. When worry threatens to cloud your mind, remember that he offers you peace and clarity. He is a faithful and kind father who wants your heart to be light.

Faithful One, I trust you to do what I cannot, and I lay down the need to control the outcomes in my life. You are far more capable than I am of handling every challenge. I trust you to guide me through each one.

FEBRUARY 22

Powerful Faith

"Don't worry or surrender to your fear. For you've believed in God, now trust and believe in me also."

JOHN 14:1 TPT

Faith doesn't surrender to fear, and it doesn't give over to worry. It pushes past, knowing that God's faithfulness has the final word. There is good reason Scripture reminds us to take courage so many times. Life is full of challenges, but God has not left us ill equipped to face them. He is with us every step of the way.

Jesus is the way, the truth, and the life. You can trust him to guide you through each of your days. If you let him, he will empower you by his Spirit and comfort you when you need it. He will lovingly lead you, focusing on progress over perfection. Find peace in the fact that he will never leave you or forsake you.

Lord Jesus, thank you giving me strength in the face of fear. Give me courage to follow you even when it is difficult. Fill me with peace when I am afraid and help me keep my eyes steadily on you.

FEBRUARY 23

The Gift of Today

"Do not worry about tomorrow; for tomorrow will worry about itself. Each day has enough trouble of its own."

MATTHEW 6:34 NASB

Each day has its own challenges. It's in our best interest to not get ahead of ourselves by worrying about what tomorrow may hold. Worry is wasted energy, and it doesn't fix anything. Especially when we are operating in anxiety, we imagine problems that may never occur. While doing this from time to time is normal, it is debilitating to live in this space on a daily basis.

Jesus' wisdom is applicable in every moment of our lives. He offers us his peace in every circumstance imaginable. Instead of jumping to the future, even by just one day, let's give our time and attention to the present. God meets us in the moment each time we call on his name. He offers us grace for today. What a gift!

Lord, thank you for today. Thank you for the opportunity to get to know you more as I walk in faith. Help me remain rooted in the present and connected to your Spirit.

Time to Delight

*Delight yourself also in the L*ORD*,
And He shall give you the desires of your heart.*

PSALM 37:4 NKJV

Life is not meant to feel like an endless grind. We are not meant to live in a constant state of stress, productivity, and overwhelm. Instead, God's desire is for us to lean on his strength and operate by his grace. There is never a day when his grace is absent. He has everything we need, and he is eager to share the abundance of his resources.

Before you set about the rest of your day, take a moment to delight yourself in the Lord. Think about his wonders, his goodness, and his faithfulness toward you. Delight isn't reserved for mountaintop moments. It is cultivated in daily encounters of his presence. Spend time in grateful adoration, and trust that God will continue to meet you with the miraculous power of his mercy.

God, fill me with delight as I turn my attention toward you. You are worthy of my time, heart, and trust. I love you!

Living Water

"Blessed are those who hunger and thirst for righteousness, for they will be filled."

MATTHEW 5:6 CSB

Scripture teaches that those who trust in Jesus will have streams of living water flow from within them. Jesus is the Living Water. He quenches the soul thirst that nothing else can satisfy. He is our daily bread, feeding our hearts with the nourishment of his love. Everything we need is found in him.

When your soul feels the pangs of hunger and you experience the desperation of thirst, there is only one solution. Jesus is the only one who brings true satisfaction. You are blessed in your hunger because it leads you to the one who can fill it. There is an unending feast in his presence. Where you feel scarcity, there is only opportunity to know the overwhelming satisfaction of God's love.

Lord, satisfy my hunger and quench my thirst in your presence. I want to know the refreshing rest that only you can provide. I trust you to meet my needs and satisfy my soul.

FEBRUARY 26

Reliable and True

*The Lord is good to those who depend on him,
to those who search for him.*

LAMENTATIONS 3:25 NLT

It can be difficult to depend on others when we have experienced disappointment or rejection. No matter how flawed our earthly relationships are, there is one who never fails. He is dependable, faithful, and unchanging. He will never drop the ball or under deliver on his promises.

Look for the Lord, and you will find him. He is easy to please, and he is full of glorious light, truth, and love. He is faultless in all he does, and we can trust him. He is untainted by greed, power, or manipulation. His sacrificial love opposes the world and its systems, but it is the true way of freedom. You can find rest, peace, and confidence in his presence.

Lord, you are good to all who depend on you. I trust you, relying on your faithfulness, even when all seems lost. Be my firm foundation and my help in times of need.

Surrender

*I seek you with all my heart;
do not let me stray from your commands.*

Psalm 119:10 NIV

What does it look like to seek the Lord with everything we have? We might assume it means never thinking about anything else or retreating to a remote place with only his presence for companionship. We can look at the life of Jesus and see that this isn't accurate. He created us for community, and he wants us to have healthy relationships and balanced lives.

Your attention can be set on the Lord at all times, no matter what you are doing. Being surrendered to him is more about the posture of your heart than what fills your calendar. As you go about your days, he will direct you when you need it. Wholehearted surrender isn't about gritting your teeth and striving for perfection. It's about being open to God's leadership whenever it comes about.

Loving Lord, direct my path as I go about my day. I trust that you will guide and correct me when needed. Give me grace to hear your voice and listen with humility.

FEBRUARY 28

Daily Wisdom

> "Blessed is the one who listens to me,
> watching daily at my gates,
> waiting beside my doors."
>
> PROVERBS 8:34 ESV

God is ready to give us wisdom whenever we ask for it. If we go to the gates of God's presence every day, listening for his voice, we will find exactly what we need to face our present challenges. God's wisdom is always right on time. He knows exactly what we need, and he is eager to provide it.

You will find rest, refreshment, and perspective in the wisdom of God. Make time to listen for the voice of the Lord and create practices that cultivate your relationship with him. Spend time with him in prayer and read the Word with the expectation that he will speak to you. Apply the wisdom you learn, and you will reap a harvest of abundance.

Wise One, thank you for your Word that instructs, guides, and encourages me. Give me grace to respond when you speak to me. When I am struggling, remind me that you are eager to give me the wisdom I need.

March

"Come to me,
all you who are weary and burdened,
and I will give you rest."

MATTHEW 11:28 NIV

MARCH 1

Aligned in Wisdom

> "My God, I want to do what you want.
> Your teachings are in my heart."
>
> PSALM 40:8 NCV

The more time we spend with the Lord, the more we know his heart. The more we know his heart, the more our desires align with his. Everything he does is motivated by life-giving love. He is full of justice, truth, and peace. There is no shadow in him.

When the wisdom of God permeates our thoughts, we become more like him. We walk in his ways because they are clear to us. This isn't to say we never misstep or make mistakes. There is grace for our failures, and we don't need to be afraid to mess up. As we get to know God more, we will reap the benefits of walking in his ways. When we need guidance, he is always near and ready to teach us.

God, I want to do what you want. Please give me grace to follow in your footsteps. Give me wisdom as I read your Word and look to your Spirit for guidance.

MARCH 2

Never Lacking

*Even the strong and the wealthy grow weak and hungry,
but those who passionately pursue the Lord
will never lack any good thing.*

PSALM 34:10 TPT

When our eyes are focused on what we lack, we miss the abundance of what is already ours. Our desire for more is highlighted by looking at the lives of others. Perhaps we look at the wealthy and long for the privilege of resources that meet more than our basic needs. Maybe we see the family dynamics of others and wish we had what they have.

Envy leads you away from rest. It also distracts you from the goodness you already have. Turn your attention to the Lord. In his presence you will see that he satisfies all your needs. Take the opportunity to write a list of gratitude today. List everything you can think of, from the ordinary to the extraordinary, and thank God for his faithfulness toward you. Every good thing is a gift from the Lord!

God, I confess that I am easily distracted by desire for more. I don't want to lose sight of the power of your provision in my life. Open my eyes to see the blessings in my life and fill my heart with gratitude.

MARCH 3

Beloved

*"I am my beloved's,
And his desire is for me."*
SONG OF SOLOMON 7:10 NASB

As God's people, we are beloved. We belong to him, and he profoundly belongs to us. His covenant with us is unbreakable. The power of his love is unlimited. Everything he does comes from the foundation of love he has for his creation. We are the object of his greatest affection.

There is confidence in knowing you are loved. Think of the strongest and surest relationships in your life. How does the strong connection of love and support impact the way you live and feel? In Christ, you have the strongest bond of love you will ever know. It is always available, flowing into our hearts and building the strength of our identity as God's beloved.

Lord, I want to grow in confidence of your love. I'm so thankful that I am yours and you are mine. Draw me close to your heart and give me assurance of my identity in you.

MARCH 4

God's Work

God is working in you, giving you the desire and the power to do what pleases him.

Philippians 2:13 NLT

When we think of God's work we might gravitate toward the big things. With breath, imagination, and the power of his word, God made the world. While creation is miraculous, he didn't stop working when the world was set. He continues to work in our hearts and lives. If we overlook his daily and seemingly small work, we will miss opportunities to strengthen our faith.

When we surrender our hearts before the Lord, his Spirit moves in us and makes his home within us. We become temples of the living God. As we follow his leadership, we will see his work in our lives. Every step we take in faith honors him. It doesn't matter if we think it's small or insignificant. He equips us to follow him, and he gives us the grace to obey him.

God, thank you for the powerful work of your Spirit in my heart and life. Thank you for your faithful leadership. Give me grace to see your work in my life.

MARCH 5

Right on Time

The Lord does not delay his promise, as some understand delay, but is patient with you, not wanting any to perish but all to come to repentance.

2 Peter 3:9 CSB

When we wait on the promises of God, it can seem like some drag on forever. We may be tempted to lose hope, but God's timing is different from our own. He accounts for factors that we don't see. Even when his timeline doesn't line up with ours, he is still working.

As children, our patience is thin. We want what we want, and we don't always see the value of waiting. However, parents know the importance of timing. As God's children, we can grow to trust our perfect Father. He has not forgotten a single promise he has made, and he will be faithful to follow through on each one.

Perfect Father, I don't always understand your timing, but I trust you. Thank you for moving in my life even in seasons of waiting. Increase my confidence in your plans and help me honor you as I wait.

MARCH 6

Well Resourced

This same God who takes care of me will supply all your needs from his glorious riches, which have been given to us in Christ Jesus.

PHILIPPIANS 4:19 NLT

All children of God have access to his glorious riches. Through a relationship with Christ, we are considered heirs to God's abundant kingdom. He is so generous to us, and we can be generous to others. We can give without worry as we confidently rely on God's faithful provision.

The same God who provided bread in the desert and water from a rock for the Israelites is the one who provides for our every need. From the beginning of time, God has provided for his people. His provision in our lives doesn't always look how we want, but nonetheless we can trust him. As he graciously gives us what we need, we can partner with him by giving to others.

God, thank you for your provision in my life. Give me a spirit of generosity and help me bless others as you have blessed me. Show me opportunities to share what you have given me.

MARCH 7

My Beating Heart

*The poor will see and be glad—
you who seek God, may your hearts live!*

PSALM 69:32 NIV

There is hope for all who look to the Lord and rely on his help. Our hearts come alive in the hope of his love. Our minds are refreshed in the beauty of his wisdom. There is joy for all those who trust in Christ Jesus, for he is the author and perfecter of our faith.

Can you remember a time when your heart came alive in the goodness of God? Perhaps it felt lighter than it had in some time. Maybe you're longing for that lightness even now. There is good news for you today. God is the lifter of your head, and there is goodness for you here and now. Put your hope in God, for he will not fail you!

Glorious God, the light of your love makes my heart bloom. Shine on me and lift my head. As I turn my eyes toward you, I trust you to give me what I need.

MARCH 8

Rooted in Relationship

"If you remain in me and follow my teachings, you can ask anything you want, and it will be given to you."

JOHN 15:7 NCV

When we are connected to the Lord in a loving relationship, we can bring him whatever is on our hearts and minds. God is a loving Father who gives good gifts. As his children, we know that he will provide for us. He will not turn us away when we call on him, and he will not shame us for bringing our messes to him. We are safe, known, cared for, and welcome in his presence.

God wants you to feel safe bringing your heart to him. He doesn't expect you to filter through your thoughts and emotions. He knows exactly how to handle your heart, and he can do that best when you bring him the most honest version of yourself. He will never ridicule you for giving him your heart. He is the safest place to land at all times and in every season.

Lord, I give you my whole heart. Thank you for being merciful and gracious when I come to you. Give me confidence to ask for what I need and trust that you know best. Align my heart with yours today.

MARCH 9

Draw Near

Be not rash with your mouth, nor let your heart be hasty to utter a word before God, for God is in heaven and you are on earth. Therefore let your words be few.

ECCLESIASTES 5:2 ESV

We've all been in situations where one person seems to take up all the space by talking over everyone else. Instead of listening, they cut others off with a quick retort or to share their own opinion. This type of communication doesn't foster connection or intimacy because it's only focused on one person.

The way of Christ is slower, gentler, and wiser. Scripture teaches that it's better to listen than to speak. It's better to have an open and curious heart, both before God and others. There is wisdom in staying quiet and seeking to understand the people around us. We can reflect God's love to the world by deliberately listening to people with patience, kindness, and intention.

Father, I don't want to spend all my time talking. Help me develop the humility needed to be quiet. May my words reflect your love and may my ability to listen show others that I care about them.

MARCH 10

Priceless

> "Listen! Are you thirsty for more?
> Come to the refreshing waters and drink.
> Even if you have no money,
> come, buy, and eat."
>
> ISAIAH 55:1 TPT

In a world where costs are continually rising, it is astounding to realize that the love of God is free. His grace and salvation are gifts we don't have to pay for. They are not cheap, but they are priceless. This is overwhelmingly good news!

What are you thirsty for today? There is satisfaction in the presence of the living. He is eternally faithful, and his peace is beyond what the world can offer. Riches cannot buy what he longs to give you. He has all you need, and you can find satisfaction, hope, and peace in him. Run to the refreshing waters of his presence and drink all you need.

Lord, thank you for the satisfaction I find in your presence. There is nothing worth pursuing more than you. I come to your living waters and drink deeply of your plentiful peace.

MARCH 11

Abundant Goodness

*He has satisfied the thirsty soul,
And He has filled the hungry soul with what is good.*

PSALM 107:9 NASB

There is abundant goodness available in every moment. No matter where we are or what our circumstances look like, God is faithful and present. We can rest in his goodness and trust him to give nourishment to our soul. We don't have to wait until tomorrow to experience his life-giving peace.

God is with you right now. In this very moment, his love can permeate your heart, soul, mind, and body. Bring your hungry heart to his table, and he will give you exactly what you need. He knows what is best, and he is infinitely aware of you. As you run to him with your need, he will meet you with abundant mercy and grace.

Present One, thank you for your attention. You are what I need right here and now. I know you will provide all I need through your grace.

MARCH 12

Heartfelt Peace

"Peace I leave with you, My peace I give to you; not as the world gives do I give to you. Let not your heart be troubled, neither let it be afraid."

JOHN 14:27 NKJV

The power of Christ's peace is beyond what we can imagine. We often limit God to our human experience, but his ways are far beyond anything we've experienced. Peace as we know it cannot be compared to God's peace. While worldly peace is temporary, God's peace is eternal. Worldly peace is manufactured and dependent on circumstances, but God's peace is unchanging and steady despite the chaos around us.

God's peace cannot be taken away. It cannot be revoked or stolen. No one can diminish the peace of God as it rules in our hearts and minds. It is freely given and generously offered to all who seek it. Praise God for the power of his peace that calms our chaotic thoughts and brings restoration to the desolate areas of our hearts, lives, and world.

Prince of Peace, you offer what no one else can. Fill my heart with peace and guard me against the empty promises of the world.

Life-giving Perspective

The mindset of the flesh is death, but the mindset of the Spirit is life and peace.

ROMANS 8:6 CSB

There is power in the words we speak. Everything we say is an overflow from our hearts. The good news is that we are not bound by the state of our hearts. Through the power of his Spirit, God can transform the way we think and feel. We aren't stuck in our thoughts, beliefs, or expectations. Even if we've developed unhealthy patterns, God can bring restoration.

As you set your mind on Christ, you are filled with the love, joy, and peace of his Spirit. When you feel despair and fear dragging you down, set your mind on God and ask for his help. There is no reason to keep thinking destructive or negative thoughts. There is life and peace for all who lean on him.

Holy Spirit, direct my thoughts, my heart, and my actions. I trust your leadership and know you will guide me with wisdom and grace. You can turn mourning to dancing, fear to courage, and graveyards to gardens.

MARCH 14

Prayerful Antidotes

Don't worry about anything; instead, pray about everything. Tell God what you need, and thank him for all he has done.

PHILIPPIANS 4:6 NLT

The world will always provide plenty of opportunities to worry, but we are not meant to stay in a constant state of stress and anxiety. Let's take every care, fear, and reasonable projection before the Lord. He welcomes it all and offers us peace in exchange.

God is a faithful provider, a loving father, and a devoted friend. He is the wisest counselor and most reliable confidant. He doesn't ask us to filter between reasonable and unreasonable worries. He is ready and waiting for us to bring him all of our cares and fears. When we do, he offers us the steadiness of his unchanging love.

Faithful Father, I don't want to waste away in worry. Give me courage to bring every anxious thought to you. Clear the cobwebs from my mind and bring me clarity and peace. I trust you to handle the things that cause me stress.

MARCH 15

Bringing Calm to Chaos

God is not a God of disorder but of peace—as in all the congregations of the Lord's people.

1 Corinthians 14:33 NIV

God does not cause confusion. He doesn't cause division or hate. He lovingly brings all things together in his peace. He does not use his power to manipulate, gaslight, or separate. His sacrificial love is equally available to everyone. Unity is created when we each fully surrender our lives and hearts to his purposes.

We cannot force others to choose peace. We can only choose for ourselves whom we will serve. We are responsible for our own homes and hearts. If we desire peace and unity, we must start with ourselves. It isn't right to expect behavior from others that we aren't willing to embrace. As we humbly welcome God into our hearts, he will calm the chaos and give us grace to bear fruit.

Father, thank you for the reminder that you are a God of order, peace, and clarity. I rest in your unchanging nature. Give me grace to reflect your peace to the world around me.

MARCH 16

Sing Your Song

*"Behold, God is my salvation;
I will trust, and will not be afraid;
for the LORD God is my strength and my song,
and he has become my salvation."*

ISAIAH 12:2 ESV

What song is in your heart for the Lord today? How has God's faithfulness astounded you? How has his grace empowered you? Take some time to meditate on his goodness and let your heart bask in the light of his glory.

The song of your heart isn't limited to one emotion. We sing dirges at funerals, celebratory songs for victories, and anthems for courage. What kind of song is ringing in you right at this moment? You might be in the midst of grief, elation, disappointment, or confusion. Whatever it is, offer it to God. Don't judge it or try to change it. Offer God the honesty of your true song and let it be your sacrifice of praise today.

Lord God, I give you the song of my heart today. Take what I have to give and fill me with peace. I trust you with the vulnerable parts of my heart.

MARCH 17

Beauty of Blessings

"May the Lord bless you and keep you.
May the Lord show you his kindness
and have mercy on you.
May the Lord watch over you
and give you peace."

Numbers 6:24-26 NCV

Offering the Lord a prayer of blessing is a powerful way to lift up the people around us. It's also a beautiful way to connect with the Lord and his heart for us. As we read today's verse, we can see various attributes of God shining through its message. God's peace, kindness, mercy, and care are available to all who seek him.

You don't have to earn God's attention or love. They are readily accessible and freely offered from his heart to yours. May you know the incredible kindness he extends in every moment. May you know the miraculous mercy of his faithfulness. May you rest in the confidence of his care, knowing he watches over you. May you know the persistent peace of his presence.

Lord, I turn my attention to the power of your nature. You are kind, patient, gentle, and true. You are consistent and caring. You are my peace.

MARCH 18

Pure Wisdom

Wisdom from above is always pure, filled with peace, considerate and teachable. It is filled with love and never displays prejudice or hypocrisy in any form and it always bears the beautiful harvest of righteousness!

JAMES 3:17-18 TPT

Worldly wisdom is different from godly wisdom. Where the world is judgmental and argumentative, God's wisdom is gentle, kind, and patient. The world's wisdom can be harsh, and it leaves little space for nuance. However, there is so much room in the wisdom of God. It is pure, peaceful, considerate, and humble.

When you prioritize the wisdom of God, you will be better for it. You don't have to play along with the rules of corrupt systems. When the world encourages you to be angry, you can embrace peace. When the world encourages you to be critical or full of rage, you can embody God's quiet and persistent love. There is no reason to fear or feel overwhelmed when you are faithfully walking in the loving wisdom of Jesus.

Lord Jesus, you embody wisdom. I choose to follow your example. You are the way, the truth, and the life. May my thoughts and interactions with others reflect your character.

MARCH 19

Humble Hearts

Humble yourselves under the mighty hand of God, so that He may exalt you at the proper time, having cast all your anxiety on Him, because He cares about you.

1 PETER 5:6-7 NASB

Though the world might not value humility, God always does. Humility is a sign of wisdom. Pride refuses to admit any weakness, but humility has a clear understanding of limitations and strengths. Pride insists on its own way, taking up as much space as it can, while humility makes room for others at the table.

Prideful people see everything as a competition, while humble and confident people know they don't have to compete for their worth. When we trust that God takes care of us, we can cheer for others while also waiting on our own moments of victory. Embracing a life of humility is a beautiful way to reflect Christ's love to others.

God, thank you for reminding me that there is room for everyone at your table. Show me opportunities to embrace humility and reflect your patient love to everyone around me.

MARCH 20

Beauty to Come

*"You shall go out with joy,
And be led out with peace;
The mountains and the hills
Shall break forth into singing before you,
And all the trees of the field shall clap their hands."*

ISAIAH 55:12 NKJV

As long as you live, there is hope. There is the promise of beauty, strength, and joy. Even when your body begins to fail, there is the anticipation of being with God for eternity. When you pass from this short life to the next, there is incomparable glory waiting for you!

Take heart in the promises of God. He says that you will go out with joy and be led with peace. The mountains and the hills will break forth in song before you, and nature will join their melody! God offers you so much beauty and goodness. His kingdom is full of abundance for all who enter it. Lean on the faithful love of God and wait with expectation for his promises to be fulfilled.

Beautiful One, you are my hope, and my heart comes alive in your presence. Thank you for the promise of beauty to come. I trust you!

MARCH 21

Values over Rules

The kingdom of God is not eating and drinking, but righteousness, peace, and joy in the Holy Spirit.

ROMANS 14:17 CSB

The kingdom of God is defined by his values rather than the rigid rules of humanity. Jesus proved this with his life and ministry. Jesus healed the sick rather than turning them away. In the eyes of the Pharisees, he broke the Sabbath rest. Christ's ability to love wasn't limited by the rules of man. He operated by the spirit of the law rather than the rigidity of it.

We can follow Jesus' lead by prioritizing the same things he did. His life was defined by righteousness, peace, and joy in the Holy Spirit. Do our actions lead us further into love and freedom? Or are we bound to a checklist that values restriction over relationships? Instead of striving for our own righteousness, let's diligently follow Jesus who is the fulfillment of the law.

God, may the values of your heart become the values my life is defined by. Protect me from legalism and pride. May my actions reflect your love to everyone around me.

MARCH 22

Room for Forgiveness

Make allowance for each other's faults, and forgive anyone who offends you. Remember, the Lord forgave you, so you must forgive others.

COLOSSIANS 3:13 NLT

Perfection is an impossible standard. We are all human, and we will fail and falter. We will disappoint others and be disappointed. It is important that we leave room for each other's humanity and make allowances for our faults. Forgiveness is necessary on the path toward connection.

God doesn't hold us to impossible standards, so let's approach others in the same way. As we have been forgiven, we can forgive others. Forgiveness doesn't mean we refuse honest conversation or stuff down our emotions. We can be honest about our hurt and also choose to forgive. If we ask him, God will give us the grace to do it.

Merciful Father, I don't want to take my freedom for granted or refuse to offer others what I've so willingly received. Lead me in love and help me be gracious to those around me.

MARCH 23

Follow His Lead

God blessed the seventh day and made it holy, because on it he rested from all the work of creating that he had done.

GENESIS 2:3 NIV

Rest is holy. It is not an afterthought in God's plan. It is an intentional and important part of it. Your body and mind both need rest. You need rest to refresh your perspective and restore your strength. Make space in your schedule for creativity, relaxation, and renewal.

Your day of rest is for you. You get to decide what activities are life-giving. Try spending time outside or curled up with a good book. Call a friend you've been missing or put your hands in your garden. Take a nap or watch a favorite movie. Whatever you do to rest, know that you are following the Lord's lead and doing what is holy!

Holy Lord, thank you for the reminder that rest isn't simply important, it's necessary. When I feel guilty for resting, remind of your perspective. Teach me how to incorporate rest into my life.

MARCH 24

A Quiet Life

Make it your goal to live a quiet life, minding your own business and working with your hands, just as we instructed you before.

1 Thessalonians 4:11 NLT

It is not wrong to aspire to live a quiet life. Wisdom is found in minding our own affairs and keeping our energy directed toward our own responsibilities. When we spend too much time judging the lives of others, we lose satisfaction and vision for our own lives.

Don't let the world convince you that your small ambitions are wrong. Little wins can feel groundbreaking. They are the reward of focusing on our own part in the great orchestra of life. Don't look to the right or to the left. Set your eyes on Jesus and confidently walk along the path he has chosen for you.

Lord, show me your plans for my life. Help me adjust my priorities and expectations. I don't want to strive for anything that isn't meant to be mine. Help me focus on the path you've chosen for me.

MARCH 25

Whispers of Wisdom

The quiet words of a wise person are better than the shouts of a foolish ruler.

ECCLESIASTES 9:17 NCV

Wisdom has no need to shout. It doesn't have to speak over others or drown out differing perspectives. It is full of patient assurance and quiet confidence. How often do we rush to interject while someone else is still speaking? Instead of getting louder, let's endeavor to listen and speak thoughtfully.

Wisdom's power isn't found in its volume. The whispers of wisdom are as powerful as any shout of defiance. It's important to remember that God's ways are different from the world. We don't have to fight fire with fire. We can ground ourselves in the gracious example of Christ and live by his wisdom instead.

Wise One, I confess I am still learning the power of a gentle answer and a listening ear. Whisper your words of wisdom to me today. Give me grace to follow Jesus' example of peace and patience.

MARCH 26

Undisturbed Peace

> The one who always listens to me
> will live undisturbed in a heavenly peace.
> Free from fear, confident and courageous,
> that one will rest unafraid and sheltered
> from the storms of life.
>
> PROVERBS 1:33 TPT

If we want to dwell in the peace of Christ, we cannot ignore the wisdom of his kingdom. We cannot let fear drag us from the path of his love. We see in part, but God sees everything fully. Why would we insist on our own way instead of trusting the one who orders our steps and clears our path?

The peace of God frees you from fear and gives you courage in the face of challenges. You can rest without fear of the future. You can find shelter from the chaos of the world as you remain rooted in the wisdom of God's kingdom. It's never too late to align your life with the peace of Christ. Today, you get to choose if you will live by peace or fear.

God, your wisdom is better than the solutions of the smartest among us. I trust you above all else. Fill me with peace as I follow you.

MARCH 27

Spirit Strength

"Not by might nor by power, but by My Spirit,"
says the LORD of armies.

ZECHARIAH 4:6 NASB

The ways of the Lord are a mystery to humankind. In his wisdom, God approaches each situation perfectly. He might not operate how we think he should, but we can have confidence that his plans are reliable and good. Instead of fitting God's work into a formula, we can lean in and have faith in his unchanging character.

God's Spirit is able to do more with one whisper than we could do with all our might and strength. We don't have to burn ourselves out or strive to accomplish God's plans. There is power in and trusting his faithful nature to follow through on his promises. Let's admit our weakness and lean on the strength of God's Spirit no matter what we face!

Holy Spirit, thank you for the power of your presence and the wisdom of your ways. I trust you to do what I cannot. Instead of pushing myself to the limit, I step back and rest in your faithfulness.

MARCH 28

Spirit of Truth

"I will pray the Father, and He will give you another Helper, that He may abide with you forever—the Spirit of truth, whom the world cannot receive, because it neither sees Him nor knows Him; but you know Him, for He dwells with you and will be in you."

JOHN 14:16-17 NKJV

The Holy Spirit is not a consolation prize for believing in Jesus. The Spirit is God's very presence, teaching us the wisdom of the kingdom, and producing the fruit in our lives. If we want to follow God with a surrendered heart, we must embrace living by the Spirit. He is the one who teaches, encourages, corrects, and guides us.

Salvation is not the culmination of our faith. Following God is meant to permeate our lives beyond our initial act of surrender. After laying down our lives at the cross, we must live by the Spirit. He dwells in us, leads us in the love of Christ, and comforts us in our suffering. As we submit to him and follow his prompts, he fills our lives with fruit.

Holy Spirit, thank you for the power of your presence in my life. Illuminate the truth of God's wisdom as I welcome your leadership in my heart, mind, and life. Thank you for your faithful guidance.

MARCH 29

Invite Him In

> He said to them, "It is I. Don't be afraid." Then they were willing to take him on board, and at once the boat was at the shore where they were heading.
>
> JOHN 6:20-21 CSB

When you invite God into your life, he will faithfully guide you. The path might not look the way you hoped, but you can be assured that he knows what he is doing. God knows what is best, and he will keep your steps steady if you trust him. Look to him for guidance, and he will not lead you astray.

You don't have to be afraid of God's plans for you. He isn't a puppet master who coerces you into doing things you don't want to. He is better than any friend you have known, and he is capable of seeing you through each of your days. His motivations are pure, and his heart is for you. The more you know him, the more you will see how wonderfully kind and gracious he is.

Lord, I loosen my grip on control and invite you into my life in a deeper way. I have tasted and seen your goodness, and I trust that you will continue to guide me. Take the lead, Lord.

MARCH 30

Even in the Dark

Even when I walk through the darkest valley,
I will not be afraid, for you are close beside me.
Your rod and your staff protect and comfort me.

PSALM 23:4 NLT

We cannot avoid dark valleys of life. None of us have perpetual mountaintop experiences of victory and joy. Though we cannot control the season we are in at any given moment, we can know the comfort of God's leadership. He will never leave or forsake us. There is no darkness he cannot navigate.

God is close beside you in this moment. Just as the gentle prodding of the shepherd reminds the sheep of his presence, so God's rod and staff comfort and protect you. You can rest in the presence of God knowing he will never abandon you. He is especially close in the darkest moments of your life. Don't be afraid because your good shepherd is nearby.

God, give me a revelation of your nearness today. I need courage, hope, and peace. Wrap me in your arms and comfort me in your presence.

MARCH 31

Faithful to Forgive

If we confess our sins, he is faithful and just and will forgive us our sins and purify us from all unrighteousness.

1 John 1:9 NIV

Authenticity matters to God. In order to receive from him, we have to be honest with ourselves and with others. If we want to experience the transformative power of his love, we must be willing to admit where we fall short. If we can't recognize our immense need for him, we won't fully surrender our lives into his hands.

God is faithful and just to forgive our flaws and failures, and he purifies us from all unrighteousness. By his grace, we are set free from the sin that entangles us. We are no longer limited by our weakness. Instead, we are empowered by mercy and grounded in love. All we have to do is confess our flaws and receive what he offers.

Faithful Father, help me face my weakness with courage and bring it to you time and again. Thank you for the powerful redemption of your love!

April

In peace I will lie down and sleep,
for you alone, Lord,
make me dwell in safety.

PSALM 4:8 NIV

APRIL 1

Not in a Hurry

Do not overlook this one fact, beloved, that with the Lord one day is as a thousand years, and a thousand years as one day.

2 PETER 3:8 ESV

Surely you have felt the crunch of time at one moment or another. When the bills are due, the window of opportunity is closing, or the time with a loved one is drawing to a close, time can feel like it's working against us. While we may struggle to have peace in the moment, God is not worried, rushed, or behind.

Consider this very moment. Do you have what you need? Air, food, water, companionship, the ground beneath your feet? The Lord is present, and he is faithful, abundant, and gracious. There is peace in his presence here and now. Trust that he will not let you go or overlook you. He will do all that he sets out to accomplish.

God, I'm so grateful that you are unchanging and steady. Thank you for your past, current, and future provision. When I want to rush your timing, help me rest in trust. You will not fail!

APRIL 2

Blessed Assurance

> I said to myself, "Relax,
> because the LORD takes care of you."
>
> PSALM 116:7 NCV

Faith is strengthened and hope is bolstered when we remember how God has already moved in our lives. Taking note of his past provision reminds us that he will continue to provide for us. This is exactly what the psalmist did in Psalm 116. He reminded himself that God had taken care of him before, so he could be confident in the future.

How has God helped you before? Lean on his proven faithfulness when you are worried or afraid. Remember that he never changes. If he has taken care of you before, he will do it again. His involvement in your life doesn't have an expiry date. He has promised to be with you every step of the way until the very end.

Lord, you have been so faithful to me. Refresh my memory and help me rest in the steadiness of your character. Give me peace that surpasses understanding and help me trust you more.

Partial Understanding

Now we see but a faint reflection of riddles and mysteries as though reflected in a mirror, but one day we will see face-to-face. My understanding is incomplete now, but one day I will understand everything, just as everything about me has been fully understood.

1 Corinthians 13:12 TPT

When we only see in part, it can be difficult to imagine the whole. Graciously, the Lord settles our hearts and minds in the perspective of his wisdom. He can help us see from a different vantage, reminding us that there is so much more at work than we naturally notice.

Until the time comes when we understand all things in the fullness of God's presence, let's continue to trust the one who doesn't miss a thing. He sees every detail and attends to every need. His love meets us in the midst of everything we experience. Even when we cannot understand what he is doing we can know the peace of his presence.

Wise One, thank you for the reminder of how little I know. Bind me close to your heart and shift my perspective. Give me wisdom and peace to navigate whatever I face today.

APRIL 4

Path to the Father

"I am the way, and the truth, and the life; no one comes to the Father except through Me."

JOHN 14:6 NASB

If we want to know the Father, we must come through Christ. He is the way, the truth, and the life. He is the open door to the presence of God, and he reveals God's nature and purposes. Jesus is the best and only way for us to gain the inheritance God intended for us. Through Christ, we know God.

Jesus revealed what the Father is like. They are not in conflict with one another. Jesus' compassion revealed the mercy and kindness of the Father. His humble attitude revealed the graciousness and gentleness of the Father. The more you get to know Jesus' character, the more you know the heart of God.

Heavenly Father, thank you for sending Jesus to save us and reveal what you are genuinely like. Thank you that I can know you through fellowship with your Son.

APRIL 5

Perfect Love

There is no fear in love; but perfect love casts out fear, because fear involves torment. But he who fears has not been made perfect in love.

1 JOHN 4:18 NKJV

The perfect love of God pushes out fear. Fear makes us act rashly, but the love of God creates space for us to dwell in peace. We can make our choices with clarity and a quiet spirit knowing that God is faithful and his love for us is never-ending. We can stay calm in the midst of chaos knowing God is steady and unchanging.

The perfection of love does not mean the removal of hard circumstances or decisions. There is a deep well of peace in the presence of God, allowing us to endure trials with his help. Without fear we can face every circumstance with confidence even when things don't go our way. We can persevere through storms because God's love is our anchor that never fails.

God, you are all the confidence I need. Your ways are better than mine, and I choose your love over fear. Keep me steadily anchored in love through the storms of life.

APRIL 6

Consistent Response

> "Ask, and it will be given to you. Seek, and you will find. Knock, and the door will be opened to you. For everyone who asks receives, and the one who seeks finds, and to the one who knocks, the door will be opened."
>
> MATTHEW 7:7-8 CSB

Ask, seek, knock. These active directives lead us to the grace of God. Those who ask receive. Those who seek find. Those who knock have the door opened. We don't stand around and wait for our turn to reach God. He is always accessible and waiting for us to move toward him. As we do, he responds!

The pursuit of God is active. We are meant to seek him with everything we have. We are promised that our efforts will always be rewarded. We don't stand at a closed door and knock until our knuckles bleed. God opens the door every time we ask. There is power in our intentional pursuit, and there is rest in the faithfulness of God's response!

God, I approach you with intention, and I trust you to answer. Thank you for responding whenever I come to you. Give me grace to pursue you with confidence.

APRIL 7

Multiplied Peace

My child, never forget the things I have taught you. Store my commands in your heart.

PROVERBS 3:1 NLT

When we store God's wisdom in our hearts, we experience the compounding goodness of his nature in our lives. Scripture says if we follow his ways, we will live many years and have a satisfying life. The quality of our lives goes up as we incorporate loyal love and kindness into the fabric of our decisions. This is how we find favor with God and people.

The wisdom of God is not arbitrary. It is helpful and useful for every part of our lives. There is peace for those who walk in the shadow of the Almighty. Let's align our choices with the heart of God's truth, for it will never steer us wrong.

Father, I trust your wisdom and your ways. I follow along the pathway of your sacrificial love and surrender my heart to your leadership. Thank you for the peace that meets me as I do!

APRIL 8

The Good Shepherd

"I am the good shepherd. The good shepherd lays down his life for the sheep."

John 10:11 NIV

Jesus is the ultimate servant leader. He surrendered his body, but before that he surrendered his glory when he came to earth dressed in humanity. He bridged the gap between us and the perfection of God. Jesus revealed the love of God, the power of God, and the person of God in a way that we could see, know, and understand.

Jesus wasn't just a good man. He was and is the Son of God. He performed miracles in his ministry, but he also lived an incredibly normal life. He relates to us in our own experiences of humanity. He understands what it means to be hungry, tired, and grief ridden. No matter what we are walking through, Jesus can comfort us and guide us through it.

Good Shepherd, I trust you as my defender, guide, and comforter. Thank you for revealing the love of God in a way I can understand. Thank you for laying your life down for me!

APRIL 9

Engraved

Behold, I have engraved you on the palms of my hands; your walls are continually before me.

ISAIAH 49:16 ESV

God sees us right where we are, and he knows what each of our days will look like. He sees our limitations, and he has a clear perspective of the problems we face. He is as familiar with our lives as he is with his own body. We are carved in the palms of his hands.

There is encouragement for your soul and strength for your body in the Word of God. There is powerful peace in his presence. God sees you, beloved. You are not alone, and he is always aware of you. You don't have to compete for his attention, and he does not see you as a burden. Join your life with his and take heart in his care of you!

God, I am so grateful that you see me, know me, and care for me. You are aware of every part of my life. Thank you for reminding me of your closeness.

APRIL 10

Faith to Believe

Know and believe today that the Lord is God. He is God in heaven above and on the earth below. There is no other god!

Deuteronomy 4:39 NCV

What does it look like to know and believe that the Lord is God? How can we put our faith into action? Perhaps a good place to start is by reading about the mothers and fathers of faith. Hebrews 11 recounts the faith of those who came before, but it begins with a definition of faith. It says that faith means having confidence in the things we hope for even without physical evidence.

We can bolster our faith by learning about God's character and paying attention to the way he operates. We can also be encouraged by his faithfulness in our own lives. We don't have to know what tomorrow will bring to trust the one who is constant today and every day. There is no other god who passionately pursues his people with loyal love and unending grace!

Lord, you alone are worthy of my devotion. What you have done before, you will do again. Strengthen my faith as I follow you.

APRIL 11

Inseparable

> Can anything ever separate us from Christ's love? Does it mean he no longer loves us if we have trouble or calamity, or are persecuted, or hungry, or destitute, or in danger, or threatened with death?
>
> ROMANS 8:35 NLT

There is no possible way to escape the love of God. This isn't a threat, but a beautiful and powerful promise. Nothing can diminish his love. When we are confident of his kindness, no trouble, hardship, or problem can separate us from his presence. We are secure in his love because his love is unchanging.

God is love, and he is always present with us. Even if we are faithless, God's love remains. We cannot be separated from the love of God because we cannot be separated from God himself. We have been brought into fellowship with him through the sacrifice of his Son. Jesus' sacrifice was enough for all time. Nothing stands between us and the glorious love of the Father.

God, what a relief to know that I cannot escape your love. Thank you for the security it gives me and the comfort I find in it. When I am overwhelmed, remind me of your all-encompassing love.

APRIL 12

Chosen

*"You whom I have taken from the ends of the earth
And called from its remotest parts,
And said to you, 'You are My servant,
I have chosen you and have not rejected you.'"*

ISAIAH 41:9 NASB

God doesn't promise a pain-free life, but he promises to never leave us in the ups and downs. He faithfully works all things together for the good of those who love him. This doesn't mean that everything looks like rainbows or victory laps. It means that as his chosen and beloved children, we have the blessing of knowing we are never alone.

When you are going through the wringer, how do you stay grounded and at peace? Whether or not life is unsettling for you at the moment, you can stand confident in the perfection of God's perspective. He sees and knows everything. He has chosen you, and he is lovingly aware of you at all times.

Creator, I am yours because you created me to be yours. I have already yielded my life to you, but I choose today to remember that I am not alone.

APRIL 13

Holy Teacher

"The Helper, the Holy Spirit, whom the Father will send in My name, He will teach you all things, and bring to your remembrance all things that I said to you."

JOHN 14:26 NKJV

We don't have to hoard information and worry about whether or not it stays ingrained. We can trust the Holy Spirit to bring to mind whatever we need. Our goal is not to cultivate perfection, but it is to develop the ability to lean on his guidance and instruction. Having a growth mindset is far more important than checking off a to-do list of habits.

There is so much grace in the leadership of God. The Holy Spirit teaches us all things, and he brings to mind truth when we need it most. He reminds us of Scripture exactly when we need to hear it. He knows what we need to navigate each of our days. As we open our hearts to his leadership, we can rest in his wisdom and perfect timing.

Holy Spirit, teach me the ways of God, and lead me into greater trust, peace, and love. I am your student! Give me grace to be obedient to your voice.

APRIL 14

Absolutely Nothing

"Nothing will be impossible with God."

LUKE 1:37 CSB

We come up against our limits every single day. We all know how it feels to be hungry, experience exhaustion, or get stuck on a problem we cannot solve. When we come up against the boundaries of our humanity, God doesn't tell us to push harder. Instead, he asks us to rely on his power, and to let go of the need to prove ourselves.

You don't have to do anything to prove yourself worthy of God's help. You can rest peacefully knowing that the one who is faithful to his Word will deliver on each of his promises. Situations that are impossible for you to figure out are not difficult for God. He is not limited by your weaknesses. He sees opportunities where you see closed doors.

God, thank you for the reminder that nothing is impossible with you. I trust you to do what only you can, and I lean into your peace while I wait.

APRIL 15

Restful Qualities

All of you should be of one mind. Sympathize with each other. Love each other as brothers and sisters. Be tenderhearted, and keep a humble attitude.

1 PETER 3:8 NLT

God's ways are higher than ours. His kingdom is defined by peace, love, and joy. It is revealed through compassionate encouragement, support, and humility. God's ways are true, and they are full of loving-kindness. The more we commit to following the Lord and his ways, the more rest our souls will know.

There are many different ways to live a life, but what matters most is that our actions reflect God's values. Every interaction we have is an opportunity to share God's love. Instead of offering prideful criticism, we can sympathize with those who are experiencing hard times. Instead of holding on to offenses, we can forgive one another and overlook each other's faults.

Father, help me be honest and open in my relationships. Give me grace to have a tender heart and humble attitude. May the way I treat others reflect your love.

APRIL 16

Faithful God

The Lord is faithful; he will strengthen you and guard you from the evil one.

2 THESSALONIANS 3:3 NIV

God surrounds us with his present peace, and he offers us the cloak of his compassion. His faithfulness covers us each and every moment. We can trust him, for he won't abandon us even for a second! His Word is reliable, and we can stand firmly on his promises. If he says he will guard us, he will.

Whenever you feel exposed or threatened, God offers the strength of his presence. Vulnerability does not have to mean danger, but instead it can be a reminder to trust in the one who is stronger than you. Rather than depending on how you feel, stay rooted in what is true. God will strengthen and guard you when you ask him to.

Faithful Lord, you are my strength and my shield. You never lift your hand from my life. You are my confidence, peace, and hope. I am surrounded by your faithfulness.

APRIL 17

Grace Gifts

By grace you have been saved through faith. And this is not your own doing; it is the gift of God, not a result of works, so that no one may boast.

EPHESIANS 2:8-9 ESV

There is absolutely nothing we can do to earn God's love. Our attempts to make ourselves better aren't what captures God's attention. Our tally of successes and failures isn't how God determines our worth. There is nothing we can do to become more or less worthy of his grace. Salvation has been given freely, and we only need to receive it with humility and thanksgiving.

We are often our harshest critics, pushing ourselves to do more and be better. We feel guilty when we don't measure up, and we set impossible standards that can never be met. This is not how God wants us to live. His desire is that we rest confidently in the work he has already done. He paved the way for us to be redeemed. Our response to his gracious gift is all that matters.

Gracious God, protect me from striving to meet my own standards of perfection. I submit to your grace, receiving it with open arms and allowing my heart to rest in your presence.

APRIL 18

Every Good Thing

Every good action and every perfect gift is from God. These good gifts come down from the Creator of the sun, moon, and stars, who does not change like their shifting shadows.

JAMES 1:17 NCV

Don't overlook the goodness in your life as a fluke. Every beautiful moment is a gift from God. Every prayer answered is a display of his love. He deserves the credit for every good thing you've ever experienced. Your life is made up of hundreds and thousands of gifts all orchestrated by your generous Father.

When you see the fruit of the Spirit at work, God is there. Whenever you experience peace, joy, hope, or gentleness, God is present. Practice turning every good moment into an opportunity of praise. There is nothing so mundane that it is not reflective of God's nearness. He is present in the seemingly boring parts of our lives as much as he is present in the miraculous.

Creator, thank you for the sun shining on my face. Thank you for the laughter ringing in the air. Thank you for this moment. Fill me gratitude for the many good gifts you have given me.

APRIL 19

Real Things

Keep your thoughts continually fixed on all that is authentic and real, honorable and admirable, beautiful and respectful, pure and holy, merciful and kind. And fasten your thoughts on every glorious work of God, praising him always.

PHILIPPIANS 4:8 TPT

Anxiety prevents us from living in our present reality. It keeps us from seeing things as they are and pulls us toward imagined outcomes. There is a reason Scripture encourages us to focus our attention on the Lord in prayer. Prayer brings us back to the present moment, offering God what we can't control, and bringing our attention to what is authentic and real.

If we are going to use our imaginations to jump ahead, let's make sure our thoughts are rooted in the assumption of God's faithfulness. We may not know how God will move, but we can trust his reliable character. He will keep each of his promises. In the meantime, we can look for the fingerprints of his mercy in our lives and in the world around us.

Lord, I praise you for all you have done and all you have yet to do. Help me turn my attention to you and focus on your goodness. Keep my mind from wandering toward anxiety.

APRIL 20

Renewed Mind

Do not be conformed to this world, but be transformed by the renewing of your mind, so that you may prove what the will of God is, that which is good and acceptable and perfect.

ROMANS 12:2 NASB

We are not victims of our thoughts or bound to our current perspective. In fact, we were created to grow and change. Our minds are incredibly flexible, and it's wrong to think we can't adjust our thought patterns when they don't line up with God's. Our thoughts dictate our actions, and God has given us the tools we need to change the way we think if needed.

If you have dealt with anxiety, you know the power thoughts can hold. Even when you feel stuck in your thought patterns, a renewed perspective is available in God's presence. As you spend time with him and dwell on his Word, he will change the way you think. The more truth you have hidden in your heart, the easier it is to think about things rightly.

God, thank you for the hope of a renewed mind. I want to see the world and my circumstances the way you do. Give me grace to store your Word in my heart.

APRIL 21

Our Source of Being

He is not far from each one of us; for in Him we live and move and have our being, as also some of your own poets have said, "For we are also His offspring."

ACTS 17:27-28 NKJV

Jesus is like oxygen to our souls. His love is like the sun, reaching us wherever we are. We need him more than we will ever understand. There is no shadow that can hide us from his presence. He is with us, and he sustains us. He is the giver of life, and he is our wonderful defender, provider, and teacher.

As God's children, we don't have to wonder where we stand with him. We are made in the image of the one and only God. He is the author of kindness and the very source of life itself. He fills our lungs with breath, and he orders our steps. He offers us the fullness of life and eternal security. As his beloved children, we have the blessing of thriving in his peace, delighting in his joy, and blooming in his love.

God, you are my Creator and Savior. Everything my soul needs is found in you. Thank you for sustaining me and filling my life with your goodness.

APRIL 22

Unwavering Help

"Because I, the LORD, have not changed, you descendants of Jacob have not been destroyed."

MALACHI 3:6 CSB

God is unchanging. He does not waver from his lovingkindness. Though the world is full of destruction, atrocities, and suffering, God remains compassionate and merciful. The presence of pain does not mean God is not near. He is always intervening on behalf of his people even when we don't understand how he is doing it.

The Old Testament is filled with stories of how God moved in the lives of his people. He faithfully led the Israelites to the promised land despite their tendency to wander away from him. If he was faithful then, he will be faithful now. He has not changed. He is the same God who looked at Israelites unfaithfulness and chose to be merciful anyway.

Unchanging God, I trust you even though I have questions and frustrations. I don't understand what is going on in the world, but I know you are in control. Give me peace as I follow you.

APRIL 23

More Than My Own

*I know, Lord, that our lives are not our own.
We are not able to plan our own course.*

JEREMIAH 10:23 NLT

Our lives are not our own. We do our best to plan our steps and make the right choices, but we do not know what tomorrow will bring. Security and confidence are found when we put our lives in God's hands and trust him to lead us. He knows what is best, and he is capable of intertwining every detail of our lives.

The God who breathed life into dry bones is the same God who leads you. Find rest in his presence today. He sews the details of your life together with the thread of his mercy, and he never fails to bring beauty out of ashes. If you are following him, you can trust that goodness and love will remain with you. He will keep your soul anchored in his presence no matter what your circumstances look like.

Lord, you are the giver of life, and I trust you. Protect me from insisting on my own way. Give me grace to humbly accept your instructions and honor you with the way I live.

APRIL 24

Refreshing Wisdom

*The law of the Lord is perfect,
refreshing the soul.
The statutes of the Lord are trustworthy,
making wise the simple.*

Psalm 19:7 niv

The wisdom of God is like a cool breeze that refreshes the overwhelmed soul. It clears the chaos and brings order out of confusion. God's ways are key to thriving in life, no matter the season, situation, or setting. As we follow his standards, he blesses us with the confidence and assurance of his presence.

Whatever you need today, God has wisdom to meet you right where you are. He offers solutions when you cannot see them. He has the ability to inspire you, shift your thinking, and equip you to do the right thing. His leadership is always gentle, kind, and rooted in his loyal love. He will show you the way to walk, and he will give you grace to do it well.

God, I need wisdom right now. You can see my life clearly, and you alone know what is best. Show me the right steps to take and give me grace to be obedient. I trust the path you've chosen for me.

APRIL 25

Trust His Hand

"I will turn the darkness before them into light, the rough places into level ground."

Isaiah 42:16 esv

Obedience begins with humble submission to God's leadership. Believe in the Lord Jesus and all he offers, and you will be saved. He has already done the work of closing the gap between humanity and God. He is the door to salvation and unhindered fellowship with the Father.

Take the outstretched hand of Jesus today. He will lead you, even when you do not know the way. He will guide you on a pathway that is marked with peace and security. He will light up the darkness before you and show you each step as you take it. As you follow him, he will smooth the rough places and guide you into his goodness.

Good Shepherd, I offer you my hand and my trust. As I move, show me the next step to take. Keep my eyes focused on you and guide me according to your Word.

APRIL 26

The Piercing Word

God's word is alive and working and is sharper than a double-edged sword. It cuts all the way into us, where the soul and the spirit are joined, to the center of our joints and bones. And it judges the thoughts and feelings in our hearts.

Hebrews 4:12 NCV

God's Word has the precision of a scalpel in the hand of a skilled surgeon. As we read it, we can either embrace it as a gift or shy away from it in discomfort. At different times we will be convicted, encouraged, or filled with hope. If we believe that each Word is alive and good, we must be willing to let it have its full effect in our lives.

The Word is sharp, but it is a life-giving tool rather than a weapon. It cuts away fear and bitterness. It removes that which holds us back from living in the liberty of love. It is not meant to be shot like arrows at the masses, seeking to harm others and put them in their place. It is a healing instrument for bringing life and awareness to our hearts and minds.

God, may your Word cut away what does not align with your kingdom. Teach me how to humbly accept what you say and live according to Scripture. Thank you for teaching me with so much grace, kindness, and gentleness.

APRIL 27

Beloved Child

The Holy Spirit makes God's fatherhood real to us as he whispers into our innermost being, "You are God's beloved child!"

ROMANS 8:16 TPT

Your life is not a mistake. You were not brought into this world on a reckless whim. You were created with intention and knit together in love. No matter the origin of your family system, you can rest assured that you are a beloved child of the Most High. He says that you are wanted, and he is proud to welcome you into his family.

As God's beloved child, you can trust him to father you well. As you spend time with him, you will grow in confidence of his affection. He sees your successes and failures and loves you all the same. He knows your strengths and weaknesses and embraces you fully. You can always be yourself when you are with him. He sees you, understands you, and knows what is best for you.

Father, thank you for assuring me of your love. I am yours and you are mine. Without you I would be lost and alone.

APRIL 28

Embodied Truth

"You search the Scriptures because you think they give you eternal life. But the Scriptures point to me!"

JOHN 5:39 NLT

We aren't saved by words. We are saved by sacrificial love of Christ. This is important to distinguish especially when it comes to wielding the Word of God. Jesus Christ is the living expression of the Word of God. Truth and love are intertwined in the person of Jesus Christ. He is the embodiment of all that is right and true.

Many people have used Scripture to excuse their offensive attitudes. Scripture is a tool; it is not God himself. Scripture points us to God, testifying about Christ and revealing the power of his salvation. Everything we do should be measured against the love of Christ. It isn't right to use Scripture to bolster our perspectives without being rooted in love.

Jesus, you are the way, the truth, and the life. You are love incarnate, and your ways are right and true. May my life reflect your love above all else.

APRIL 29

Strength in Waiting

Those who wait on the LORD
Shall renew their strength;
They shall mount up with wings like eagles,
They shall run and not be weary,
They shall walk and not faint.

ISAIAH 40:31 NKJV

Sometimes the answer to feeling desperate isn't to push harder; it's to take a step back and wait. When anxiety propels us to do more, it can feel counterintuitive to stop for a moment. Instead of dwelling in our frenzied thoughts, we often need space to breathe, think, and connect to the source of true peace.

Doing more, trying harder, and pushing ourselves beyond our capacity is not healthy. None of those things are the answer to peace, joy, or contentment. What we really need is a direct connection to the well-spring of God's grace. He is the only eternal source of peace. Any feelings of satisfaction that we muster up will not last beyond our time on earth. When we depend on God for renewal, we are promised unending life and satisfaction.

Lord, help me rest in your presence rather than striving for success on my own. Instead of surrendering to anxiety, I surrender to you.

APRIL 30

Powerful Renewal

If anyone is in Christ, he is a new creation; the old has passed away, and see, the new has come!

2 CORINTHIANS 5:17 CSB

In Christ, all things are made new. This includes our souls, bodies, and all of creation. We live in the tension of knowing that the world doesn't look the way it's supposed to. We endure the suffering of this age knowing that one day Jesus will make all things new. We long for the day when his perfection is our reality.

When you surrendered at the cross and declared Jesus your Savior, your old self passed away. Praise God for the hope that comes from knowing you are a new creation. Let the joy of your redemption fill you with anticipation for the future and complete redemption that is coming. Jesus has made your soul new, and one day everything around you will follow suit.

Lord, thank you for the promise of renewal in your presence. Thank you for giving me new life and filling me with hope. Give me a fresh revelation of how you have redeemed me.

May

You will keep in perfect peace those whose minds are steadfast, because they trust in you.

ISAIAH 26:3 NIV

MAY 1

Fresh Perspective

Let the Spirit renew your thoughts and attitudes.
EPHESIANS 4:23 NLT

In order to let the Spirit renew our thoughts and attitudes, it's important to consider the old way that we've left behind. Scripture says we are supposed to throw off our old sinful nature and follow Jesus' ways instead of being ruled by lust and deception.

We were not designed to constantly search for personal satisfaction. Christ has shown us a new way to live. By the power of his Spirit, we can humble our hearts before him and receive his love. The more we dwell on truth, the more we are able to change our thoughts and attitudes. As God shifts the way we think, our actions and behavior will follow.

Holy Spirit, you are my teacher. Lead me with wisdom and renew my thoughts and attitudes. Transform the way I think and help me honor you with my actions.

MAY 2

Restored Joy

*Restore to me the joy of your salvation
and grant me a willing spirit, to sustain me.*

Psalm 51:12 NIV

God doesn't expect us to be happy all the time. His presence doesn't mean an absence of pain or suffering. However, we can access the deep well of his joy no matter what is going on in our lives. We can find satisfaction in his presence even when our circumstances are a mess.

God loves to remove the weight of our worries and bless us with his unrelenting peace. When we surrender our hearts and minds to him, he restores the joy of his salvation. He reminds us of what really matters, and he keeps us grounded in the truth. He relieves our fears, and he gives us grace to endure whatever we are currently facing.

Gracious God, restore to me the joy of your salvation and grant me a willing spirit. Draw me closer to your heart and sustain me today. Help me trust you no matter what my day looks like.

MAY 3

Inner Renewal

We do not lose heart. Though our outer self is wasting away, our inner self is being renewed day by day.

2 CORINTHIANS 4:16 ESV

Even while our bodies give out, our inner selves can experience renewal in the presence of God. He fortifies our hearts and gives us courage to face the day. Our bodies will not always cooperate or do what we hope they will, but God's strength within us will never fade.

God dwells within us, and he empowers us to follow him. Through the Holy Spirit we can have constant fellowship with the Lord. Every moment is an invitation for renewal. No matter how we perceive things physically, spiritually we are on the path to eternal life.

Holy Spirit, thank you for making your home in me. Strengthen me from the inside out and give me endurance to follow you all my days.

MAY 4

Persistent Mercy

*The Lord's love never ends;
his mercies never stop.
They are new every morning;
Lord, your loyalty is great.*

LAMENTATIONS 3:22-23 NCV

There are no limits to God's kindness. There is no possibility of running out of his mercy. Each day is an opportunity to receive more of God's love. No matter what the previous day looked like, today's mercy is new and endlessly available.

Thank God that his faithfulness is never-ending. No matter the state of the world, the never-ending love of God is present. There isn't a chance you could run out. God's love is even more persistent than the dawning of the sun. Will you open your heart to receive it as it meets you?

Merciful Lord, I open my heart to you today. Flood my awareness with the power of your love just as it is and right as it meets me.

MAY 5

Our Coming Hope

> "He will wipe away every tear from
> their eyes and eliminate death entirely.
> No one will mourn or weep any longer.
> The pain of wounds will no longer exist,
> for the old order has ceased."
>
> REVELATION 21:4 TPT

Today's verse speaks of what is yet to come. When Jesus rules and reigns on earth there will be no more tears, threats of violence or death, or mourning what has been lost. The earth along with all those who dwell in the light of God's salvation will be wholly restored.

It is hard to imagine a time without pain, stress, or suffering. We may become weary while we wait, but we have the presence of God to remind us of our hope. On our worst days we are fueled by the promises that will be fulfilled. No matter how much we suffer now, our eternity will be filled with God's powerful presence and overwhelming glory.

King of kings, I long for the day when every wrong thing will be made right. Strengthen me while I wait for that glorious day. May your kingdom come, and your will be done, on earth as it is in heaven.

MAY 6

Empowered Living

I have been crucified with Christ; and it is no longer I who live, but Christ lives in me; and the life which I now live in the flesh I live by faith in the Son of God, who loved me and gave Himself up for me.

GALATIANS 2:20 NASB

When we surrender to Christ, we gain far more than we give up. We receive miraculous salvation, gracious love, and freedom from sin and death. In Christ there is peace, joy, and eternal hope. There is grace, kindness, and encouragement. There is more abundance than we can imagine in his glorious kingdom.

Each of us can know the power of Christ within us. As we walk in the wisdom of his ways, we experience the Spirit's help at every juncture. There is strength for our weakness. There is hope for our disappointment. There is restoration for what we've lost. There is so much goodness in his fellowship.

Spirit, your presence empowers me to live in the fullness of God's love. Thank you for giving me strength to be generous, kind, patient and honest. Your ways are better than the ways of this world.

MAY 7

Hearts of Compassion

I will give them an undivided heart and put a new spirit in them; I will remove from them their heart of stone and give them a heart of flesh.

Ezekiel 11:19 NIV

When you think of a stony heart, what comes to mind? Is it apathy or cold disregard? Perhaps you imagine a stubborn or prideful person who distances themselves from others. Maybe you think of a stingy or grumpy person. The truth is a stony heart can lead to many attitudes. It remains inflexible and cut off from compassion. The only remedy for a hard heart is the healing and redeeming mercy of Christ.

God's love melts our hearts and gives us new life. He transforms us when we surrender our lives to him in humility. As his love permeates our hearts, we begin to feel the compassion of God's heart for others. It motivates us to value connection over isolation, unity over dissension, and compassion over striving for success. A heart of flesh that is surrendered to the Spirit grows the fruit of the Spirit.

Lord, I don't want to be cold and distant. I don't want to withhold kindness and readily dole out judgment on others. Your law of love keeps my heart soft. Thank you for the unifying power of your love.

MAY 8

All Together

> Put on your new nature, and be renewed as you learn to know your Creator and become like him. In this new life, it doesn't matter if you are a Jew or a Gentile, circumcised or uncircumcised, barbaric, uncivilized, slave, or free. Christ is all that matters, and he lives in all of us.
>
> COLOSSIANS 3:10-11 NLT

Jesus Christ is the great unifier, and he lives in all of us. There is no distinction between ethnicity, background, language, or class in his kingdom. There are only followers of Christ and children of God. When we allow our differences to create distance between us, we miss the all-encompassing love of God.

God created each person to reflect His love and creativity. What a wonderfully diverse world this is, with different customs, cultures, and expressions of God's glory. Resist the desire to categorize yourself and others. Instead look for the things that unify us. We are all brought together in Christ.

Creator, thank you for the reminder that your love unifies and doesn't divide. I want to know the power of your love that binds us together.

MAY 9

Strength for Today

I can do everything through Christ, who gives me strength.
PHILIPPIANS 4:13 NLT

Sometimes the rest we need is found in the courage we gain in God's presence. We can relax when we realize that God is in control, and everything he does is for our good. No matter what we face, God is with us. No matter what we go through, Christ is our present strength. It doesn't matter how strong or weak we feel. God is near, and he is our help.

Memorize today's Scripture coming back to it time and again throughout your day. Anything that is required of you can be achieved with the strength of Christ. Through him you are fully equipped to face the days, weeks, and months ahead. Move forward with the expectation that there is nothing too stressful or difficult for God to manage. He is on your side, and he is eager to help you.

Lord Jesus, help me live to the fullest no matter what I have to do today. I lean on your strength. You are my courage, and I find my rest in you. I surrender to control to you, and I trust you to lead me.

MAY 10

Making a Way

> "Forget the former things;
> do not dwell on the past.
> See, I am doing a new thing!
> Now it springs up; do you not perceive it?
> I am making a way in the wilderness
> and streams in the wasteland."
>
> ISAIAH 43:18-19 NIV

Reflecting on the past is natural to us. However, when we dwell on it too often, it keeps us from embracing the present. It also keeps us from looking toward the future with hope and anticipation. It's okay to reminisce and learn from the past, but what matters most is what God is doing right now.

God always makes a way. You can count on it! He is the God who creates life in desolate places and straight paths through the wilderness. It doesn't matter how barren or wild your current season is; God will make a way. You don't have to long for what used to be. As a child of God, you can be confident that the best is always yet to come.

Father, I trust you to do what only you can. Fill me hope for the future and keep my eyes on you. When I am tempted to dwell on the past, fill me with anticipation for what you are doing right now.

MAY 11

Faith to Keep On

Everyone who has been born of God overcomes the world. And this is the victory that has overcome the world—our faith.

1 JOHN 5:4 ESV

Faith gives us gives us eyes to see what is not yet in our hands. With faith we believe that God will fulfill each of his promise. While fear causes us to doubt and worry, faith encourages us and gives us confidence. Faith is maintained not by our own striving, but through the power of the Holy Spirit.

Through faith, we overcome the world. We are equipped to be victorious against the systems and practices of the world. We are not bound to compromise, limitations, fear, and selfishness. These things are no longer our standard. Christ's kingdom, purposes, and character have become our new normal. Let's take up our faith and move in the power of God's gracious Spirit today.

Gracious God, my faith is in you. Give me grace to live according to your standards and purposes. Fill me with love, wisdom, and peace. I choose to walk in your ways rather than the ways of the world.

MAY 12

Audience of One

Do you think I am trying to make people accept me? No, God is the One I am trying to please. Am I trying to please people? If I still wanted to please people, I would not be a servant of Christ.

GALATIANS 1:10 NCV

Trying to please people is a fool's errand. It's not that we shouldn't consider others, but we cannot let our choices be dictated by what others may think of us. We will never please everyone. What one person delights in, the other may hate. It's impossible to align our lives with the opinions and preferences of everyone around us.

God's values never change. He is always good, kind, gracious, and true. While the whims of others may feel like a moving target, God's ways are set. He is steady and easy to please. His requirements of you are not a mystery or difficult to attain. Instead of trying to make everyone else happy, ask the Lord how you can honor him today.

Lord, help me differentiate between what people want of me and what you want. Awaken me to your purposes and equip me to fulfill them. Give me confidence to choose you above all else.

MAY 13

Heavenly Realities

Feast on all the treasures of the heavenly realm and fill your thoughts with heavenly realities, and not with the distractions of the natural realm.

COLOSSIANS 3:2 TPT

God's truth lightens our load and refreshes our spirit. When we apply the Word to our lives God gives us peace, relief, rest, and renewal. He brings clarity and grace. He invites us to cultivate a relationship with him instead of demanding a list of requirements.

Fill your thoughts with the treasures of God's wisdom. Meditate on that which brings peace, joy, kindness, gentleness, compassion, and hope. When you feel yourself becoming distracted by the worries of this world, turn your eyes toward the Lord. Be humble and open to adjusting your habits and priorities. Fill your thoughts with the things that cause the Spirit's fruit to grow in your heart.

Creator, fill me with wonder at all you have done and are yet to do. Keep my eyes focused on you and help me stay attuned to your voice. When I become distracted, graciously draw me back to you.

MAY 14

Liberating Truth

"You will know the truth, and the truth will set you free."

JOHN 8:32 NASB

The truth isn't like a prison cell, and we don't need to be threatened by it. There is liberation in living honestly and authentically. When we try to hide the darkest parts of ourselves, we give those parts control and inevitably allow them to impact the way we live. The truth is always the right path.

True freedom is found in following Jesus. He sets us free by the power of his sacrificial love. He redeems every part of us. He doesn't shame us for our brokenness or hold us accountable to our weaknesses. When we bring ourselves fully to the cross, we are met with abundant grace and mercy. Through faith in him we are set free.

Jesus, you are my salvation and my shield. Give me the grace necessary to live truthfully and authentically. Keep me from hiding any part of myself from you. I trust you with my whole heart.

MAY 15

When Fear Rises

> The Lord is my light and my salvation;
> Whom shall I fear?
> The Lord is the strength of my life;
> Of whom shall I be afraid?
>
> PSALM 27:1 NKJV

The Psalms contain the full spectrum of human emotion. The psalmists did not shy away from revealing how desperate they were or how deep their grief was. The experiences shared are real and relatable. The beauty of the Psalms is found in the consistency of redemption. Even when the writer starts out full of despair, by the end of each psalm there is resolution, praise, or joy despite circumstances.

We can learn from the example each psalmist displayed. We can turn our eyes toward Jesus despite our circumstances. We can feel debilitatingly afraid and intentionally choose to trust God. Even when there isn't a solution in sight, we can lift up his name and find peace in the unknown. Through every season of the soul, God is worthy of our utmost praise and devotion.

Lord, you are my salvation, and I put my hope in you. You are my strength, so I won't be afraid of my circumstances. You hold my life in your hands, so I will not be terrorized by anxiety. I am yours, and you are mine.

MAY 16

Working It Out

I am sure of this, that he who started a good work in you will carry it on to completion until the day of Christ Jesus.

PHILIPPIANS 1:6 CSB

We are all a work in progress. There isn't anyone who is an exception to this rule. As long as we are living, we have the opportunity to grow in grace, learn from our mistakes, and expand our capacity to love. None of us are stuck in our ways or incapable of being transformed further by God's grace and mercy.

Being in progress can feel disorienting at times. When life is filled with disappointments, let's remember the liberating truth that God is not done with us. He never abandons us. He strengthens the weak, heals the sick, and comforts the brokenhearted. The one who started a good work in us will carry it on to completion!

Lord Jesus, thank you for the reminder that you are not finished working in my life. I am yours, and I trust you. Have your way and encourage my heart as you faithfully transform it.

MAY 17

Strong in the Lord

Be strong in the Lord and in his mighty power.
EPHESIANS 6:10 NLT

This final word from Paul to the Ephesians wasn't an encouragement for them to tighten their bootstraps or do better. They didn't need to prove themselves or earn their place as God's children. No, the encouragement was to find their strength in the Lord rather than themselves.

What does it look like to be strong in the Lord? Paul goes on to describe the armor of God in the subsequent verses. This includes wearing truth as a belt and righteousness as body armor. Peace should be our footwear while the shield of faith puts out the fiery arrows of the enemy. Salvation is our helmet, and the Word of God is our sword. When we ask him, God equips us with all these things.

God, I want to be strong in you and in your mighty power. I partner with your purposes, arming myself by your grace alone. You are the only one who can give me what I need to stay faithful.

MAY 18

Weary Heart

*He gives strength to the weary
and increases the power of the weak.*

ISAIAH 40:29 NIV

God is gentle toward us when we are in pain. He is tender toward us when our burdens are too much to bear. He doesn't kick us while we are down, and he certainly doesn't take advantage of our vulnerability by making us feel worse. He is a gentle comforter, kind counselor, and gracious savior.

When your heart is weary, rejoice in God's kindness. Speak Scripture over yourself and remind yourself that he notices and equips those who are weak. It doesn't matter how many days, weeks, or months you have struggled. He gives strength to those who come to him. You don't have to be afraid of the reception you'll receive when you turn toward your Savior. He is gentle, powerful, and able to restore you.

Loving Lord, sometimes I forget how wonderfully kind you are. I am weary, and I need your strength. I need your love to bind my wounds and heal my hurt.

MAY 19

Every Blessing

Blessed be the God and Father of our Lord Jesus Christ, who has blessed us in Christ with every spiritual blessing in the heavenly places.

EPHESIANS 1:3 ESV

Through Christ we have access to every spiritual blessing. When we surrender our hearts to him, he gives us access to the glorious riches of God's kingdom. There is no limit to his wisdom, righteousness, grace, or mercy. As we respond to his sacrificial love, he meets us with an abundance of blessings.

Take a few minutes to notice all the good in your life right now. Every blessing you have is a gift from your maker. He has not overlooked you, and he will not fail to come through for you. There is goodness to be found in this present moment even if your circumstances don't look how you want. As you follow Jesus, every day of your life can be filled with peace, love, and hope.

Father, thank you for the gifts you've given me! Open my eyes to see your fingerprints on my life. Shift my perspective and give me confidence in your faithfulness.

MAY 20

Refreshing Rains

Let's try to learn about the Lord; he will come to us as surely as the dawn comes. He will come to us like rain, like the spring rain that waters the ground.

HOSEA 6:3 NCV

God is faithful to those who wait on him. He shows up with mercy every time. He comes like the rain watering the earth. He brings refreshment which reaches the roots of our hearts. His love gives us new life when we need it most. We flourish in him even through droughts and storms.

Is there an area of your life that feels like a drought? Perhaps you have been short on peace. Maybe you have felt stuck in disappointment. Wherever there is need, God can meet you. He will come to you as surely as dawn appears. He will create fruit from the most barren patch of dry land. Invite him into the broken parts of your heart and wait with expectation.

Lord, you are more faithful than the rising sun. You are steadfast, true, and always on time. I wait on your refreshing rains to rejuvenate and restore my life!

MAY 21

Step by Step

> Though all your wanderings wearied you,
> you never said, "I give up."
> Your strength was renewed
> so that you did not faint.
>
> Isaiah 57:10 TPT

Every day is an opportunity to know the empowering grace of God. When we offer what we have, that is a step in the right direction. Perfection is not the goal. Weaknesses in our bodies, minds, and hearts, are not an indictment against our faith. Weaknesses provide an opportunity to trust the Lord and allow his strength to help us.

You have the choice to take steps toward the Lord today. You don't have to tackle everything at once. You don't have to compile your weaknesses and attempt to overcome them as a whole. You simply need to take the next right step. God is with you as you refuse to give up. Even when following him feels less productive than you'd like, you can trust his ability to lead you.

God, I choose to follow you. My heart is entwined with yours. Show me the next right step and give me grace to listen to your voice. Thank you for leading me so perfectly.

Everyone Has a Place

There is no longer Jew or Greek, there is no longer slave or free, there is no longer male and female; for all of you are one in Christ Jesus.

GALATIANS 3:28 NASB

God's kingdom is open to all. It is not an exclusive club with requirements only the elite can meet, and it's not a hidden group that operates in the shadows. God's kingdom welcomes everyone who desires to enter it. It is a place for all to find redemption, rest, and belonging in the presence of the Creator.

How often do you separate people into categories in your mind? While it's easy to do, that is not the way of Christ or his kingdom. His kingdom is full of all who call on him in truth. It doesn't matter where we were born, how much money we make, or what we have to offer. The playing field has been leveled by his marvelous mercy. We are all recipients of his generous grace.

Father, thank you for accepting me as your own. I haven't earned your love, yet you lavish it on me extravagantly. Remind me of the unity and belonging that is found in your kingdom.

MAY 23

Gracious Fellowship

May the grace of the Lord Jesus Christ, and the love of God, and the fellowship of the Holy Spirit be with you all.

2 CORINTHIANS 13:14 NKJV

By the power of the Holy Spirit, we have consistent fellowship with Jesus. The Spirit is the one who leads us to all truth and understanding. As we engage with him and become sensitive to his voice, we will experience even greater measures of satisfaction in our relationship with God.

There is so much promise, hope, and life-giving encouragement in the fellowship of the Spirit. The Holy Spirit comforts us in our suffering, strengthens us in our weakness, and encourages us in truth. The Spirit corrects us in kindness, empowers us in gracious strength, and helps us forgive as we have been forgiven. All the help we need is found in the presence of the Spirit.

Gracious Spirit, I'm so grateful for your presence in my heart and life. Move in me today, for I am your willing vessel. Point me toward truth and strengthen my faith.

MAY 24

Where You Belong

You did not receive a spirit of slavery to fall back into fear. Instead, you received the Spirit of adoption, by whom we cry out, "Abba, Father!"

ROMANS 8:15 CSB

You are accepted, loved, and cherished by your heavenly Father. If you have opened your heart to Christ and are following his ways, there is no fear that can hold you down. There is no threat of losing your place as God's child. You can be confident in the covenant he has made with you.

God has adopted you into his family. He claims you as his own, and he offers you the covering and authority of his own name. He brings you into the fold where you have access to his wisdom, resources, and healing presence. You belong at the feasting table in his house. He has given you a place, and it cannot be taken away from you by anyone.

Father, thank you for the reminder of the confidence I find in your love. No matter where I go, your name is my covering. I belong to you.

Surefooted

> The Sovereign Lord is my strength!
> He makes me as surefooted as a deer,
> able to tread upon the heights.
>
> HABAKKUK 3:19 NLT

When the air is thin and the terrain is rough, the grace of God remains sure. The Sovereign Lord is our strength. He makes us surefooted and gives us the agility to walk on high places. There isn't a place we could go in this world where God's grace is absent.

What are you struggling to navigate today? What are you hesitating to face even though you know you must? Ask the Lord to meet you in your weakness, indecision, and need. The Holy Spirit will give you all you need. His wisdom will show you what to do when you are at a loss. Rely on his leadership throughout your day, and he will not fail you.

Lord, you are my strength and my confidence. I trust you to lead me, equip me, and help me as I go into this day. When I begin to struggle, remind me that you are my ever-present help in times of need.

Image Bearers

God created mankind in his own image, in the image of God he created them; male and female he created them.

GENESIS 1:27 NIV

Have you ever looked at people through the lens of God's love? Each person we meet is an image bearer of God. There isn't a person walking this earth who doesn't reflect his likeness in one way or another. As such, each person deserves our utmost respect and compassion.

Our differences are a delight to God. He didn't create us to be the same as each other. He doesn't want us to shrink ourselves or pretend to be something we aren't. He sees, loves, and accepts us as we are. Confidence cannot be mustered up. True confidence comes from knowing we were created with intention, purpose, and love.

Creator, give me eyes to see others and myself through your perspective. Show me opportunities to practice acceptance of myself and others.

MAY 27

Living Love

We have come to know and to believe the love that God has for us. God is love, and whoever abides in love abides in God, and God abides in him.

1 John 4:16 esv

God's love can transform every part of your heart. As you abide in him, he abides in you. His presence lights up the dark places and creates life where there is none. As you experience the transformative power of God's love, you can share it with others. You honor him when you reflect his love to the world around you.

You align yourself with God when your actions reflect his love. When you choose compassion over judgment, mercy over punishment, and peace over division, God is with you. As you operate in this way, you advance the kingdom of God on the earth. Everything God does is defined by love, and you fulfill his purposes when you prioritize love.

God, help me grow in love! Abide in me and fill me to overflowing. Show me how I can advance your kingdom on earth. I want to display your love for all to see!

Fight Temptation

> When people are tempted, they should not say, "God is tempting me." Evil cannot tempt God, and God himself does not tempt anyone.
>
> JAMES 1:13 NCV

God does not tempt us. When we feel the urge to compromise, it is never from God. He is the embodiment of truth, and there is no shadow or falsehood in him. He does not lie, and he does not shame or trick us. He isn't waiting for us to mess up, and he isn't keeping a record of how many times we fail.

God readily gives you strength to resist temptation. He is eager for you to lean on him when your biggest weaknesses threaten to overwhelm you. He has already equipped you with the power of the Holy Spirit and the Word. Fill your heart with truth, and it will come to mind when you need it most. Go into the battles of life expectant that God will fight with you and for you.

Father, I don't want to blame you for things that are not from you. Help me discern your will and give me strength to fight temptation. When I am weak, remind me of the truth.

Inner Strength

God will never give you the spirit of fear, but the Holy Spirit who gives you mighty power, love, and self- control.

2 TIMOTHY 1:7 TPT

Our response to hardship can help or hinder us. Though we may initially feel fear flooding our nervous systems, God has given us the Holy Spirit who offers us power, love, and self-control. We can feel afraid without aligning ourselves with a spirit of fear. The way we handle our fear dictates whom we serve.

The Holy Spirit can bring breakthroughs in areas where you have submitted to fear. He offers you the clarity of God's wisdom, the comfort of his presence, and the strength to do the right thing. When fear tests your heart, remember that God never leaves you. There is power, love, and self-control just a breath away.

Holy Spirit, thank you for your mighty mercy at work in my life. When fear sends me spinning, ground me in your love and give me strength to focus on the truth.

MAY 30

Lord of All

Jew and Gentile are the same in this respect. They have the same Lord, who gives generously to all who call on him.

ROMANS 10:12 NLT

In Christ, there is no distinction of religious practice, cultural background, or geographical location. There are only brothers and sisters of Christ. There are only children of God. All who call on the Lord will be saved. There is no exception to this in the law of God's love.

We don't have to like everyone in order to treat them with respect. We don't have to agree with them to honor their humanity and worth as children of God. We don't have to understand them to love them well. Jesus calls us to love all people equally without exception. His love creates unity in places where we cannot muster it up.

Lord, give me eyes to see the beauty in humanity. Give me your perspective of the people around me. Help me see the worth and value of each person I come across.

MAY 31

Signs of the Spirit

"The wind blows where it wishes, and you hear the sound of it, but cannot tell where it comes from and where it goes. So is everyone who is born of the Spirit."

JOHN 3:8 NKJV

Though the wind is invisible, its effects are obvious. Though our eyes cannot see it, we feel its cooling breeze. Hair is blown about, water ripples into waves, and trees sway. Winds can be calm and refreshing, and they can also be powerful and awe inducing.

The signs of the Spirit are not visible to the eye, but they are felt. The effects are clear. You may not be able to tell where it originates or where it will go, but you can feel the power of the Spirit when it touches your life. If you ask for a fresh perspective, God will give you eyes to see how he is working in the world. Today, be alert to the movement of the Spirit.

Lord, thank you for the power of your Spirit that moves through the earth like wind. Open my eyes to see what you are doing in my life and in the world.

June

Then God blessed the seventh day and made it holy, because on it he rested from all the work of creating that he had done.

GENESIS 2:3 NIV

JUNE 1

Enough for Today

"Give us today our daily bread."

MATTHEW 6:11 CSB

When Jesus taught his disciples to pray, he didn't lead them in long, vague prayers. He made it simple. Read the entire Lord's prayer and notice how short and to the point it is. We don't have to beg the Lord to hear our prayers. He honors our simple requests and accepts our humble worship.

When we ask, God promises to give us what we need for today. Our hearts can find rest in his faithfulness toward his people. In the desert, God provided manna for the Israelites every morning. We can trust God to provide for us in the same way. He knows exactly what we need, and he is eager to give it to us.

Provider, thank you for your faithfulness. Thank you for giving me all I need to get through today. I trust that you know best.

JUNE 2

Steadfast Compassion

*The LORD is compassionate and merciful,
slow to get angry and filled with unfailing love.*

PSALM 103:8 NLT

God's love is faithful and endless. It is always present and more than sufficient. God's patience is kind and steady. Though our patience may run thin, God's doesn't. He is slow to anger and compassionate beyond our understanding.

Let the love of God flood your senses even now as you turn your attention to the nearness of his presence. Whatever heaviness you have, God offers to exchange it for lightness and peace. His love lifts burdens and offers rest. It brings comfort, compassion, and strength. When you are sick and tired of the losses and trials of this world, turn your attention to the abundant love of God.

Lord, you are patient, merciful, and close. Fill me with your love and give me strength to face every trial and trouble. Thank you for graciously leading me through life.

JUNE 3

Friend of God

> "I no longer call you servants, because a servant does not know his master's business. Instead, I have called you friends, for everything that I learned from my Father I have made known to you."
>
> JOHN 15:15 NIV

Jesus reveals the keys of God's kingdom to all who follow him. His life is a clear reflection of God's character and purposes. Everything he did pointed back to the nature of God. Because of Jesus, God's ways are not a riddle or a mystery. God's ways are simple and true. They never deviate from the values of his unfailing nature.

If we want to truly know what God is like, we have no further to look than Jesus Christ. He is the way, the truth, and the life. When we get to know him, our eyes are opened to seeing the nature of God everywhere. Just as friends know each other, we learn to spot the fingerprints of God's mercy in the world.

Jesus, it is beyond me that you would call me friend, but I am so thankful for presence in my life. Thank you for showing me God's character and making a way for me to be with him forever.

At all Times

Trust in him at all times, O people;
pour out your heart before him;
God is a refuge for us.

PSALM 62:8 ESV

It is a wonderful relief to know that God isn't overwhelmed by the things that overwhelm us. He isn't surprised by anything. He is our peace in the midst of chaos. He is our calm in the storm. We only have to hold on and keep trusting him.

Give God your heart even when it is full of questions, doubts, and frustrations. He knows you fully, and he wants you to be authentic. You don't have to hide yourself from him, for he welcomes you with open arms. He can handle what you can't. Trust him by going to him and pouring your heart before him. Trust him by taking refuge in his presence.

Father, though my heart is feeble, I come to you with all that is in it. Give me courage to be vulnerable and authentic with you. Shelter me in your presence and give me new life as I lean on you.

JUNE 5

Heaven's Goodness

Since you were raised from the dead with Christ, aim at what is in heaven, where Christ is sitting at the right hand of God.

COLOSSIANS 3:1 NCV

When we chose to follow Jesus, his overcoming victory became ours as well. His resurrection life is also ours. There is hope, peace, and joy in the fellowship of Jesus. We are called to reflect his character and keep our eyes focused on heaven in all we do.

When we fix our minds on the realities of heaven, where Christ sits enthroned at the right hand of the Father, our hearts are put to rest. With a heavenly perspective, we can navigate the trials of this life with grace, peace, and confidence. Focusing on our eternal reality helps us endure our current one. We will steadily walk in the direction of our gaze.

Jesus, you overcame sin, shame, fear, and death. Open my eyes to your goodness and help me be more like you. Keep me focused on the reality of your kingdom rather than my current struggles.

JUNE 6

Moving Closer

Move your heart closer and closer to God, and he will come even closer to you. But make sure you cleanse your life, you sinners, and keep your heart pure and stop doubting.

JAMES 4:8 TPT

Moving closer to God isn't something we do one time. It is a continuous habit that we practice even as we falter. When we fall, the Lord lifts us again and shows us how to move forward. He graciously teaches us how to follow him, and he never refuses us when we move toward him.

We cleanse our lives by removing all the things that hinder love. We forgive, for our own sake and for the sake of others. We choose compassion, pursue peace, and stand for justice. We embrace humility and willingly admit when we are wrong. The more we move toward the Lord, the more our lives will resemble his.

Lord, I move my heart closer to you today by offering you all I am. Transform me into your likeness and show me how I can reflect your character to those around me.

JUNE 7

Humble King

Love is patient and kind. Love is not jealous or boastful or proud or rude. It does not demand its own way. It is not irritable, and it keeps no record of being wronged.

1 CORINTHIANS 13:4-5 NLT

Jesus showed us what love looks like in practice. Christ-like love is not brash or overbearing, and it does not insist on its own way. It is patient, kind, and gracious. It does not act cruelly toward others, and it is not motivated by jealousy. It doesn't seek its own way or become consumed by offense.

What areas of love would you like to grow in? Where do you see opportunities in your life to practice the love of God in new ways? Growing in love isn't always a neat process. It takes sacrifice, consistency, and endurance when you are weary. Loving others is often inconvenient and even uncomfortable. As you learn to lay your life down, God will strengthen you and give you the necessary grace.

Humble King, teach me how to reflect your love in practical ways. Show me how to humbly lay my life down for others. Today, give me endurance and perseverance in love.

Delighted In

"The LORD your God in your midst,
The Mighty One, will save;
He will rejoice over you with gladness,
He will quiet you with His love,
He will rejoice over you with singing."

ZEPHANIAH 3:17 NKJV

God doesn't look at you with pity or impatience. He sees you as the beloved child you are. It doesn't matter how old you are, you are God's child, and he rejoices over you with gladness. He is faithful to help you every time you cry out to him.

Not only is God faithful, but he is happily faithful. He loves to help you! You don't have to worry about reaching him at a bad time, for he is always full of love toward you. No matter what is going on in the world, he has time for you. There is always room in his heart for you. Let his joyful affection wash over you today.

Good Father, awaken my heart, mind, and spirit to your delight! Give me confidence in your love and affection for me. Wrap me in your arms and help me find rest in your presence.

JUNE 9

Grow in Grace

Grow in the grace and knowledge of our Lord and Savior Jesus Christ. To him be glory both now and forever!

2 PETER 3:18 CSB

The invitation for fellowship with the Lord Jesus isn't limited by time or circumstance. His offer of transformation is continuous. We faithfully follow him for all our days, and he promises to steadily unveil God's love over the course of our lives. A plant takes time to grow, thrive, and blossom, and so do we.

Each day is an opportunity to grow in the grace and knowledge of your Savior. Grace is not finite; it is limitless. There is always more room to become like Jesus. Refuse to be stagnant and cultivate an attitude of continual growth. Trust Jesus as he cuts back certain areas of your life and coaxes life out of others.

Gracious Jesus, you are the vine and my true source of life. I surrender to your expert hand. Fill me with the love of your presence and provide all I need to grow in grace each day.

JUNE 10

All for Him

Whether you eat or drink, or whatever you do, do it all for the glory of God.

1 Corinthians 10:31 NLT

We can honor God no matter what we are doing. We can reflect his character by choosing to be loving, gracious, and peaceful at all times. We don't have to be working in ministry to honor him, and we don't have to save our surrender for Sunday mornings. It's important that we understand everything is an opportunity to honor the Lord.

Every seemingly mundane part of your life can be an act of worship toward God. The way you conduct yourself and treat others matters. The way you go about your day is important. There is nothing too small to surrender to God. Allow the Holy Spirit to direct you, and he will guide, encourage, and correct you as you submit to him.

Lord, thank you for the ability to worship you at all times. I submit my heart and life into your hands. Give me grace to honor you in all I do.

JUNE 11

A Loving Response

Loving God means keeping his commandments, and his commandments are not burdensome.

1 John 5:3 NLT

The commands of the Lord are not burdensome. They are for our good. His wisdom is full of light, truth, and clarity. If we want to love God more, the way we do that is to follow his ways. When we love others the way we love ourselves, when we move in compassion, mercy, and grace, we love God well.

When a friend asks you to do something you know is important to them the loving the response is to do it. If we view God's commands in this way, it becomes easier to be obedient. We listen to his voice and follow his instructions out of love and devotion. We do it because of the strength of our relationship with him not because we are obligated.

Lord, your love is transformative and worth my whole life. I surrender to you because I trust you and believe that you will do what you say. I choose your ways because I love you!

Divine Fellowship

"I have given them the glory you gave me, so they may be one as we are one. I am in them and you are in me. May they experience such perfect unity that the world will know that you sent me and that you love them as much as you love me."

JOHN 17:22-23 ESV

Our relationship with God shouldn't be defined by independence or separation. This applies as much to people as it does to our relationship with him. We were not made to isolate ourselves or hide away from the world. One of the ways that we experience the divine fellowship Christ speaks of in today's verse is by letting our light shine for all to see.

What dims your light of love for others? What keeps you from connecting? God wants you to know the power of unity and fellowship. Look for ways to strengthen relationships in your life. Confidently operate the way God made you and trust that there is a place for you. Allow Christ's light within you to shine brightly.

Lord, I want to know the power of your unifying love. Show me how I can strengthen my relationships. I want to reflect your character to the world around me.

JUNE 13

Fruit-bearing Promises

"I am the vine, and you are the branches. If any remain in me and I remain in them, they produce much fruit. But without me they can do nothing."

JOHN 15:5 NCV

The Lord guarantees that those who remain in him will produce the fruit of his Spirit. It is his responsibility to fulfill that promise. We don't become more patient, loving, peaceful, gentle, or hopeful on our own. Striving for perfection won't result in the fruit of the Spirit. It happens as we join our lives to our Savior.

While Jesus is the vine we are joined to, the Father is the gardener. He prunes, trims, and cleans the places of our lives that need it. He does this so we will bear even more fruit than we would without his help. As we remain in Jesus, following his lead and never wandering from his love, we experience the life-giving goodness of the Father's hand in our lives.

Father, find me in your vineyard, rooted in Christ. I trust your hand to prune, clean, and trim away what doesn't serve you or your kingdom. Please fill my life with good fruit.

Attentive Father

"Don't worry. For your Father cares deeply about even the smallest detail of your life."

MATTHEW 10:30-31 TPT

Worry intensifies when we feel alone and aren't sure how things will turn out. Still, it doesn't have to rule our hearts and minds. We can know the powerful peace of God as it meets, sustains, and motivates us. There is never a time when we are truly alone.

God isn't indifferent to your struggles. He is acutely aware of every part of your life. He cares deeply about the details of your days, and he is ready and willing to help you. No matter how insignificant you think something is, God wants to be part of it. He cares for you more deeply than you can imagine.

Father, thank you for being so attentive and kind. I will rest in you today knowing you can handle all my worries. Lead me deeper into your love today.

JUNE 15

Great Mysteries

"Ask me and I will tell you remarkable secrets you do not know about things to come."

JEREMIAH 33:3 NLT

God delights in sharing his marvelous mercies, compelling wisdom, and powerful truth with all who seek him. No matter what problem we are facing, we can ask the Holy Spirit to guide us. When we find ourselves stressed, we can ask him to bring peace and clarity. He always knows what to do, and he answers those who call on him.

When you seek him, God will share the beauty of his perspective. He offers glimpses of his glory, and he willingly invites you into his story. Partnering with him is like embarking on the best adventure of your life. Each day there is more to learn and discover. Listen carefully for his voice and expect him to share remarkable secrets with you.

Great God, thank you for answering every time I call to you. Thank you for the wisdom of your Word, the transformative power of your Spirit, and the comfort of your presence.

JUNE 16

Satisfying Love

Hope does not disappoint, because the love of God has been poured out in our hearts by the Holy Spirit who was given to us.

ROMANS 5:5 NKJV

Every hope is fulfilled in the love of God. He is everything we will ever need. There is provision, peace, and power in his presence. When we devote our lives to him, we will not be disappointed. His love is worth everything we have. Any struggle we experience cannot compare to the glory of his promises.

God's love satisfies your heart like nourishment satisfies the body. His love is your source of life and your hope. You can rejoice that you are fully taken care of and provided for. Abundant goodness is yours because of who your father is. Every moment is a chance to experience the overwhelming love of God which enriches your life and promises an eternity of perfection.

Lord God, your love is unlike anything else. Satisfy my soul and fill my heart with love. Draw me closer to you and renew my hope.

JUNE 17

Covenant of Kindness

> "Pay attention and come to me;
> listen, so that you will live.
> I will make a permanent covenant with you
> on the basis of the faithful kindnesses of David."
>
> ISAIAH 55:3 CSB

We are not on a path toward destruction or nothingness. There is life for us ahead. There is hope for the fulfillment of promises. If we pay attention to God's Word, we will be confident in his covenant. If we trust what he says, we will not be let down. The God of Abraham, Moses, and King David is the same God who offers us salvation and eternal security.

God's promises don't depend on us. They depend on his faithful nature. This is astoundingly good news for us. We can never mess up God's plan. We can't avert his love or stop his mercy. His goodness cannot be diminished or removed. He will do everything he has promised!

Lord, thank you for the reminder that your covenant is sure. Your promises are based on your nature, so I know they won't fail. Give me ears to hear your voice today.

JUNE 18

Cherished Children

See how very much our Father loves us, for he calls us his children, and that is what we are! But the people who belong to this world don't recognize.

1 JOHN 3:1 NLT

God doesn't simply tolerate us. He doesn't love us out of obligation, and he isn't frustrated with us. He is not like a boss who delegates to workers and then steps back. We are his beloved children, and he longs to be close to us. He wants to have a personal relationship with each of us.

You belong in the family of God, and that means you have a place in his house. As part of his family, you can have confidence in his love for you. You belong with him, and he readily welcomes you in. His love is the foundation of our identity. The way you live is impacted by how well you understand your position as God's child.

Heavenly Father, I'm so grateful to be your child. Thank you for your love that fills my heart and gives me strength. Give me confidence in my position in your family.

JUNE 19

He Answers

"Before they call I will answer; while they are still speaking I will hear."

ISAIAH 65:24 NIV

God is faithful to answer his children. Even before we need help, God sees us. Let's take him at his word and trust him. We never need to exaggerate our faith or pretend to be confident. He is not intimidated by our doubts. We can bring him our questions and hesitations. He always meets us with mercy and grace.

God always knows exactly what you need. Before you think about asking, he is aware of your questions and concerns. His sovereignty is a wonderful source of security. You can lay down your need to micromanage your life. You can let striving cease and just breathe deeply. Allow him to do what he does best.

God, thank you for answering me when I cry out to you. Thank you for always giving me a solution, a way through, or grace to endure. Thank you for faithfully ordering my life.

JUNE 20

Author and Perfecter

We do this by keeping our eyes on Jesus, the champion who initiates and perfects our faith. Because of the joy awaiting him, he endured the cross, disregarding its shame. Now he is seated in the place of honor beside God's throne.

HEBREWS 12:2 NLT

Jesus saw what was waiting for him on the other side of the cross. He saw it, not with his physical eyes, but through the eyes of faith. He knew that he was obediently following the will of the Father and offering us a path toward redemption. His heart was sure that all the suffering would be worth it.

Jesus, the author and perfecter of our faith, didn't turn away from suffering. As a result, we can trust him with our own suffering. There is nothing so awful that it diminishes or erases the promises of God. God's faithfulness stands the test of time. Let's fix our eyes on Jesus when we need courage. He will never stop helping us!

Faithful One, thank you for enduring so much on my behalf. I don't want to grow faint in faith; I want to grow strong. You are the author and perfecter of my faith. I trust you to help me.

JUNE 21

Heartfelt Hope

"Everyone who lives and believes in me will never die. Martha, do you believe this?"

JOHN 11:26 NCV

Martha had every reason to doubt Jesus' words. Her brother had died, and they had already buried him. Her hope could have been understandably frail at that point. Even though her circumstances were difficult, she didn't hesitate in her response to Jesus. She confidently responded with resounding affirmation.

Martha testified in faith as to who Jesus was. Even in her grief and disappointment, she believed that he was who he said he was. May God give you grace to do the same. As you get to know him as a friend, may you declare the truth about who he is no matter what your circumstances look like.

Lord, my greatest hope isn't in anything I can gain or lose in this life. My confidence is firm in you. You are the one who has redeemed me and set me free. Take my life and draw me closer to you.

JUNE 22

Walk It Out

Put into practice the example of all that you have heard from me or seen in my life and the God of peace will be with you in all things.

PHILIPPIANS 4:9 TPT

Learning doesn't happen only by listening and observing. It happens by practicing what we hear and gaining experience. When we put the ways of God into practice in our lives, we truly learn what it is to be followers of God. When we actively abide in his love, we show that we are his children.

Look at the good examples in your life. Who are the people you respect? What about them garners such admiration? Pick one area you want to grow in and practice those principles. Deliberate actions coupled with perseverance will bring breakthrough as you practice what you preach.

God, give me fortitude and endurance as I practice walking in your ways. When I make mistakes, give me humility and grace to try again. With each step I take, draw me closer to your heart.

JUNE 23

Continual Change

We all, who with unveiled faces contemplate the Lord's glory, are being transformed into his image with ever-increasing glory, which comes from the Lord, who is the Spirit.

2 Corinthians 3:18 NASB

We all love stories where the underdog walks away victorious. We want to see the sick become well, the victim find vindication, and the overlooked rise to success. The beautiful truth of the gospel is that we are all in the midst of our own similar story. As believers, we are all overcoming circumstances with God's grace as we journey toward eternity.

We are in the process of becoming. Our story isn't over, yet we are promised victory. We know exactly how satisfying and perfect the conclusion will be. Even when the plot twists and turns, we know we will overcome every obstacle in the end. The Spirit is working in each of us to bring us from glory to glory. He will faithfully lead us every step of the way.

Lord, thank you for the work you continue to do in my heart and life. May the story of my life honor you. Continue to transform me in your loving presence.

JUNE 24

Royal Behaviors

Since God chose you to be the holy people he loves, you must clothe yourselves with tenderhearted mercy, kindness, humility, gentleness, and patience.

COLOSSIANS 3:12 NLT

As sons and daughters of the Living God, we represent him well when we adopt his ways and move in sync with his nature. We bring honor to his name when we display mercy, kindness, humility, meekness, and long suffering. Living according to God's standards is the best and most satisfying way to live. Not only does it give others a glimpse of who God is, but it fills our own lives with goodness and satisfaction.

The ways of God's kingdom are for the good of everyone. His expectations are not arbitrary. Everything he asks of us has a purpose, and his standards are a gift. It becomes much easier to submit to his ways when we realize there is no better way. He gives us parameters to live within because he loves us and knows what is best.

Lord, it is the honor of my life to know you and be known by you. I genuinely want to reflect your mercy, grace, and peace in my life. May my words and actions honor you.

Already There

*God is our refuge and strength,
a helper who is always found
in times of trouble.*

Psalm 46:1 csb

God is already present when troubles arise. He is in the battle with us. He is ready to help at all times! When we are completely overwhelmed by trouble, God is not shaken. He is ready to intervene on our behalf whenever we call out to him.

When you come up against a problem this week, remember today's verse. Turn your attention to the presence of God. He is already with you. Tell him what you need and trust him to answer. Give your heart to the Lord instead of giving in to worry. He will never leave you alone. He has the solutions for every challenge you face, and he longs to be involved in your life.

Gracious God, you are my help and peace in times of trouble. In all circumstances, you are close. Thank you for your constant and reliable presence.

JUNE 26

Bolstered in Hope

The Scriptures give us hope and encouragement as we wait patiently for God's promises to be fulfilled.

ROMANS 15:4 NLT

The Scriptures are a deep well of wisdom and encouragement. They offer us hope for the future and reassurance of God's faithfulness in the past. They point to Jesus who is the embodiment of the Word. They reveal the power of God, and they assure us of his never-ending love.

When you need a dose of courage, where do you turn? When your hope wavers, may you find comfort and encouragement in the Scriptures. The book of Psalms is full of validation for a wide spectrum of emotions. Proverbs shares the wisdom of God, and the Gospels reveal the life-changing message of Christ. No matter which page you turn to, there is hope interwoven between every word.

Lord, open my eyes and ears as I read your Word today. Soften my heart toward your instructions and fill me with hope for tomorrow.

JUNE 27

Reason to Rejoice

Love does not delight in evil but rejoices with the truth. It always protects, always trusts, always hopes, always perseveres.

1 Corinthians 13:6-7 NIV

Love is mindful, attentive, and thoughtful toward those who are hurting. Love doesn't stand by while others are hurt. It doesn't rejoice in violence or corruption. It doesn't endorse manipulation or turn a blind eye to abuse. Love protects, trusts, hopes, and perseveres.

You don't have to conjure up love on your own. The love of God is real, ready, and always available to you. It is a life-giving source of restoration and peace. His love for you is a precious gift. It is more valuable than anything you can muster up for yourself. May you know the life-changing and sustaining love of God today.

Savior, thank you for your love that is stronger than death. Give me a fresh revelation of your love and help me love others the way you love me.

JUNE 28

Unwavering

Let us hold fast the confession of our hope without wavering, for he who promised is faithful.

HEBREWS 10:23 ESV

Jesus is a solid foundation. He is the reason we can have steady and unwavering hope. He is our faithful rock who cannot be shaken. When we build our lives on Christ the rock, we rely on his nature, trust, and protection. Though the winds of the world may rage, and storms may come, our spiritual home remains untouchable.

God's nature is the basis of our faith. He is loyal, trustworthy, and true. He does what he says he will, and his Holy Spirit affirms the truth of his Word with the power of his presence. When the terrain of life is rough, let's turn our attention to the rock of ages. He is the only one who will never crumble or deteriorate.

Faithful One, your unchanging nature is my firm foundation. You are the rock I have built my life upon. I hold fast to this hope, for you are the ultimate promise keeper.

JUNE 29

Present Portion

I say to myself, "The LORD is my portion; therefore I will wait for him."

LAMENTATIONS 3:24 NCV

God is the bread of life. He is our daily provision and the source of our sustenance. He is our portion, and his presence brings manna for our hearts to feast upon. When we begin our day by waiting on him, we acknowledge that he alone fulfills the longing of our heart.

The more we get to know the Lord in his love, the surer we become of his faithfulness. He always comes through. He might not work according to our timelines, and he isn't bound to our whims. He knows what we need down to the smallest detail. We can trust him to meet us, provide for us, and fill us with the glorious goodness of his presence.

Lord, you are my daily bread. I know you will show up when I wait for you. Thank you for meeting me with your liberating love. You are worth waiting for.

JUNE 30

Embrace It

The promise of entering into God's rest is still for us today. So we must be extremely careful to ensure that we all embrace the fullness of that promise and not fail to experience it.

HEBREWS 4:1 TPT

God's promise of rest isn't limited by time. His promises remain powerful and effective from the beginning of history until the end. His faithfulness exceeds our timelines. He kept his word to generations past, he is currently keeping his word, and he will forever continue to do so. We can embrace what he says just as fully as the original audience did.

God's people are promised rest. Our striving can cease because Christ's work is sufficient. We don't need to earn our place with God, or work toward perfection in this life. Instead, we are promised peace, mercy, and grace. We are given the gift of eternal rest through no merit of our own but through Jesus who took our burdens upon himself.

God, thank you for the promise of rest. You are the one true God whose faithfulness spans the ages. I join my life to yours and enter into your rest today.

July

Do not be anxious about anything, but in every situation, by prayer and petition, with thanksgiving, present your requests to God.

PHILIPPIANS 4:6 NIV

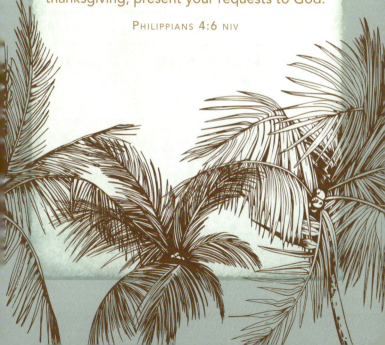

JULY 1

History of Hope

*You are my hope;
Lord God, You are my confidence from my youth.*

Psalm 71:5 nasb

Our hearts can find so much encouragement by remembering our history with God. It doesn't matter how little or how long we've spent with him. The Lord's mercy is present throughout every season. His saving grace is as powerful years in as it was in the beginning. His loyal love never changes.

Invite the Holy Spirit to bring to mind his faithfulness through the timespan of your fellowship with him. Ask him to open your eyes to his goodness even when you were not aware of it at the time. May your heart be filled with hope as you see the fingerprints of his kindness woven through the details of your life.

Lord, thank you for your faithfulness. I cannot tell you the depth of my gratitude for your ever-present love. You are my confidence and hope.

JULY 2

Your Choice

*I will look to the Lord;
I will wait for the God of my salvation;
My God will hear me.*

MICAH 7:7 NKJV

Every day presents new opportunities to decide how you will live. What choices will you make today? How will you regard yourself, and how will you interact with others? Though each day brings its own frustrations and joys, you can always choose where to direct your attention.

No one will make you wait on the Lord. If you want to you can persist through your day and be overrun by seemingly more important tasks. However, incredible grace, rest, and peace are found in his presence. When you carve out time for him, he meets you with grace and mercy. Your deliberate pursuit of God will not leave you disappointed. You will never regret the decision to put him first.

Lord, you are the God of my salvation. I choose to look to you throughout my day. Give me grace to turn my attention toward you.

JULY 3

Confident Hope

*You will be confident, because there is hope.
You will look carefully about and lie down in safety.*

JOB 11:18 CSB

Hope can be the difference between persevering and giving up. Without hope people perish. Hope is essentially looking forward to something with confidence. As believers, our great hope is in the faithfulness of God. We trust that he will keep his promises no matter what. He will redeem all of creation and make all the wrong things right.

You can put your hope in God and confidently expect that eternity with him will be worth your current struggles. You can lie down in peace knowing that God, your living hope, is close. You don't have to worry or fret. Set your eyes on him, and let him be your vision, hope, and refuge.

God, you are my greatest source of hope. I trust you to do everything you say you will. Give me peace and confidence as I wait on your promises to be fulfilled.

JULY 4

Deep Wells

If I could speak all the languages of earth and of angels, but didn't love others, I would only be a noisy gong or a clanging cymbal.

1 CORINTHIANS 13:1 NLT

The humble person has no need to shout over others or defend their position with flashy shows meant to distract or convince. The person of integrity does not need to trick anyone or elevate themselves above others. The person who is motivated by love speaks with their actions rather than boisterous arguments.

Without love, whatever we do is simply noise. Where selfish ambition creates dissention, arguments, and eventual chaos, love creates peace, unity, and life. Let's aim to be people of deep love rather than shallow shows of strength. Love is far more fruitful, and it is all that matters in the end.

Merciful God, love fuels everything you do. May my actions and words reflect your love. Keep me from pridefully insisting on my own way. Give me grace to choose the humble path of sacrificial love.

JULY 5

Better Still

"What no eye has seen, what no ear has heard, and what no human mind has conceived"—the things God has prepared for those who love him.

1 CORINTHIANS 2:9 NIV

God has prepared greater things for those who love him than we could ever imagine. It is more plentiful than what has ever been seen. It is more glorious than what any ear has heard. It is more wonderful than what any mind has imagined.

If you love God with your heart, mind, and soul, you can be sure this applies to you. That means that the best is yet to come! As a believer you are promised an eternity filled with beauty beyond your wildest dreams. There will be glory beyond your comprehension in the fullness of his kingdom. God's hand on your life now is but a glimpse of the perfection to come. There is so much more to look forward to.

Lord, thank you for the promise of perfection coming. I look forward to the fullness of your kingdom and the restoration of all things. Give me glimpses of your glory even now.

JULY 6

Well Watered

*"Blessed is the man who trusts in the Lord,
whose trust is the Lord.
He is like a tree planted by water,
that sends out its roots by the stream."*

JEREMIAH 17:7-8 ESV

Those who trust the Lord are like well-watered trees planted by streams of living water. Though the weather may change, bringing heat waves and storms alike, there is no need to fear the elements. Well-watered trees will bear fruit both in and out of season, for their very source is the Spirit of God.

Where does your trust lie? Where does your confidence come from? If your source is anything but the Lord, he invites you to increase your reliance on him. His living waters are always satisfying. His wisdom offers keys to abundance in every season of the soul. No matter where you are planted or what season you are in, you can be a well-watered tree in the garden of God.

Father, you are a good gardener. You know what you are doing, and I trust you to care for me. May your refreshing water reach the tendrils of my roots. You are my true source of life.

Fear Not

> He created you, people of Jacob;
> he formed you, people of Israel.
> He says, "Don't be afraid, because I have saved you.
> I have called you by name, and you are mine."
>
> Isaiah 43:1 NCV

The same God who created Jacob and Israel also created you. His power is as palpable now as it was in ages past. His faithfulness to us is as sure as it was to the people we read about in Scripture. God's character has not changed. When we need courage, we can let his promises be our hope.

No matter what is going on in your life or in this world, God is faithful. He is able to save you from every enemy or difficult situation. Sometimes he will alter your circumstances, and sometimes he will equip you to endure them. No matter what his hand upon your life looks like, he will rescue you. He has done it before, and he will do it again.

Powerful One, you are my courage when fear settles on my chest. I trust you to deliver me and protect me. I lean upon your proven faithfulness today.

JULY 8

By the Spirit

The "law" of the Spirit of life flowing through the anointing of
Jesus has liberated use from the "law" of sin and death.

ROMANS 8:2 TPT

While the law of sin and death condemns, the law of the Spirit offers restoration. God encourages us as he draws us in with kindness. His correction doesn't shame us; it shows us opportunities to learn and grow. We know his ways are better than ours, so we can trust that his correction is also mean for our good.

The path of love is not narrow because of its inability to save many. It is narrow because few choose to follow it. The wider path that leads to destruction is tempting with its shortcuts and empty promises. However, love is always the best and most direct route to the Father. God's ways offer you a life filled with hope. When you follow the law of the Spirit, you follow the path to freedom.

Liberator, your law of love is the law I choose to follow. Your ways are always worth it. Give me grace to stay on the narrow path of love.

JULY 9

Resurrection Life

"I am the resurrection and the life. Anyone who believes in me will live, even after dying."

JOHN 11:25 NLT

Long life is not promised to any of us. However, we are promised eternal life. The difference being that we cannot escape our humanity. We cannot outrun the clock or safeguard our health. We can strive to increase the quality of our short lives on earth, but we cannot escape death.

Our hope is not in the length of our days. It is in the glory of Christ's kingdom. It is in the fullness of life that awaits us in coming age as heaven comes to earth. There will be no more sadness, no more death, and no more separation. The resurrection and return of Christ are our hope and promise.

Savior, you are the resurrection and the life. My hope is in you, not in what I can gain or lose in this life. There is so much more awaiting me in your kingdom, and I trust that it is far better than I can imagine.

JULY 10

Sweeter than Honey

How sweet are Your words to my taste,
Sweeter than honey to my mouth!

PSALM 119:103 NKJV

God's Word is sweeter than honey. It is life-giving and satisfying. It is delicious and rich, bringing both nourishment and pleasure. When we delight in the Word, we set ourselves up for success. We benefit from the truth, wisdom, correction, and encouragement it brings. God's Word is a precious gift.

What sweet words have impacted you lately? The Word of God is not stingy, stagnant, or irrelevant. It is a rich, sweet, freshly baked portion that can delight your senses. Ask God to meet you through the Word today. He will give you grace to understand it and humility to accept it. Read it with the expectation that you will be encouraged and inspired.

Lord, your Word is like honey; it is sweet and satisfying. Fill me with an even greater desire for it. Give me grace to understand what I read.

JULY 11

Pleasant Words

Pleasant words are a honeycomb:
sweet to the taste and health to the body.

PROVERBS 16:24 CSB

God's Word is like honey, and the words we speak to one another can have the same effect. They taste sweet on the tongue and offer health benefits to the body! With this in mind, we should choose wisely how we speak. The things we say can have a positive or negative impact on the people around us.

You get to decide how you will speak. Each day is filled with opportunities to communicate with love and kindness. Choose pleasant words that uplift others and create light in the darkness. Speak with intention, purpose, and wisdom. Even when hard truths must be shared, consider how you can do so with the same compassion God has toward you.

Father, I want others to expect pleasantness and kindness from me. I don't want to be known as someone who complains, puts others down, or speaks negatively. Help me control my tongue and inspire me to speak in a way that honors you.

JULY 12

Greatest of All

Three things will last forever—faith, hope, and love—and the greatest of these is love.

1 Corinthians 13:13 NLT

There is no limit to faith, hope, or love. Scripture says they are endless resources that go on forever. As such, there is no need to limit them in our lives. We don't need to love sparingly, hope only on certain occasions, or put boundaries on our faith. There are lots of things in life that run out, but faith, hope, and love never will.

There is always enough to go around in God's kingdom. Our faith can always increase. Our hope doesn't have any limits. Our love can always be replenished. There is no threat of running out of any of these things. In every situation, there is an abundant supply of faith, hope, and love to meet our needs.

God, your kingdom is overflowing in resources. Thank you for offering me limitless faith, hope, and love. When I am discouraged, remind me you have all I need in excess.

JULY 13

Your Anchor

This hope is a strong and trustworthy anchor for our souls. It leads us through the curtain into God's inner sanctuary.

HEBREWS 6:19 NLT

Hope is an anchor in the unpredictable sea of life. It keeps us steady while the winds and storms of life come and go. The anchor of hope reaches beyond what we can see and into the very presence of God. Even when our circumstances seem impossible, hope in God is our rescue.

When you feel like you're in over your head, the anchor of hope holds firm. You can use it at any time to plant your heart in the steadfast faithfulness of God. He will not let you go. He will not let you drift off course. He will not let you become lost. Trust him and feel the strength of hope steadying you even now.

Lord, you are my safest place, and I trust you. Hope is the anchor that grounds me in you. When storms come, remind me that I will remain steady in you. No matter how much the waves rock me, I won't drift away.

JULY 14

Hold Fast

Let love be genuine. Abhor what is evil;
hold fast to what is good.

ROMANS 12:9 ESV

Romans 12 outlines a practical definition of a follower of Jesus. Be reading it, we see that above all else our lives should be defined by love. Love is what empowers us to turn away from evil and hold fast to what is good. Without love, we would be bound by a list of rules and requirements.

Genuine love is humble, considerate, and kind. It does not shrink from the honest truth. It doesn't ignore corruption, violence, or hatred. Root yourself in the nature of Christ and spend time in the lavish love of his presence. He will fill you with all that you need so that you have plenty to give others. The more you experience his genuine love for you, the more you can do the same for the people around you.

Lord Jesus, you are the source of all that is good and true. I choose to follow you, holding fast to your love. Give me grace to live according to your law of love.

JULY 15

Salvation's Song

The LORD gives me strength and makes me sing;
he has saved me.
He is my God, and I will praise him.
He is the God of my ancestors, and I will honor him.

EXODUS 15:2 NCV

Have you ever experienced such relief that it made you want to sing? This is what today's verse illustrates. Moses and the Israelites sang this song after fleeing Egypt. God saved his people, and they responded by worshipping him and lifting up his name.

Yesterday's victory is today's offering of praise. Don't glaze over the good things God does in your life. It's easy to focus on the negative, but God is worthy of your praise through every season of the soul. Don't run to him only when you are struggling. Take note of his goodness and offer a song of thanksgiving to him whenever something comes to mind.

Lord, today I will sing you a new song, straight from my heart to yours. Thank you for your presence, salvation, and unwavering help in my life.

The Golden Rule

"The way you want others to treat you is how you should treat everyone else."

Luke 6:31 TPT

Giving others the benefit of the doubt increases our compassion and kindness. Assuming the best of others is a practical way to share the love of Jesus. We innately want others to do the same for us, so we should practice the habit as well. Even when it's difficult, God gives us grace to value people as he does.

You can't control how other people treat you, but you can control your response. Instead of fighting fire with fire, you can choose to embody the gracious and merciful love of Christ. If you are wrong about something, you don't want to be berated. If you make a mistake, you don't want it thrown in your face. Love others with the same patience and dignity you desire from them.

Jesus, help me be gracious, kind, and forgiving toward others. Help me be patient enough today to take the time to consider how I want to be treated. When I rush to judgment, help me choose differently.

JULY 17

Cloud of Witnesses

Since we are surrounded by such a huge crowd of witnesses to the life of faith, let us strip off every weight that slows us down, especially the sin that so easily trips us up. And let us run with endurance the race God has set before us.

HEBREWS 12:1 NLT

If you've ever run a race, you know the power of encouragement. The cheers heard at the finish line can spur you on to persevere even when you've pushed yourself past your limit. The steady voices urging you to keep going give you strength in the midst of weakness. They remind you of your ability, and they give you something good to focus on.

The life of faith can feel lonely at times. There are times when it feels weary to stay on the narrow path. Today's verse is a reminder that we are not alone. Here on earth, we have a worldwide community of believers, and in heaven we have the testimonies of those who have gone before us. Their stories can strengthen us to endure. When you feel your faith waning, remember that there is a great cloud of witnesses cheering you on.

Lord, thank you for the power of community. When I need endurance, remind me of those who have gone before me. You faithfully led them across the finish line, and I trust you will lead me too.

JULY 18

It Will Work Out

All things work together for good to those who love God, to those who are the called according to His purpose.

ROMANS 8:28 NKJV

Sometimes our lives feel like puzzles that are missing a couple pieces. We feel disheartened when we can't see how things line up. When something unexpected happens, we are discouraged that it doesn't fit into the big picture. When we are overwhelmed by stress, we struggle to see how everything will come together.

The Lord is incomparably wise. He takes the details of our lives and weaves them together into the tapestry of his mercy. There isn't anything we need to worry about. He is capable of bringing restoration to even the direst of circumstances. He knows exactly how the puzzle fits together. All we have to do is trust his steady, creative, and expert hand.

God, I love you. I struggle with worry when it comes to the unknowns in my life. I trust you, so give me grace to follow you closely. I believe you will create beauty where I cannot.

JULY 19

People of Peace

> "Blessed are the peacemakers,
> for they will be called sons of God."
>
> MATTHEW 5:9 CSB

The children of God are recognized by their actions. We reflect the powerful nature of our heavenly Father when we choose to pursue peace. Jesus has shown us the way to the Father. He revealed how to live through his own life. He was powerfully humble and peaceful, and he asks us to mirror his character.

Choosing to make peace instead of causing dissention is not always natural. It certainly isn't always the popular choice. However, it is the way of Christ. There is joy in making peace, for it settles the tension and creates pathways through the wilderness. Being a person of peace is a powerful choice that aligns us with the heart of the Father. His house is ruled by peace, and his ways are always best.

Lord, I want to build peace. Teach me how to pursue it and offer it to others. Give me grace to be a peacemaker in all situations. Thank you for helping me grow in this way.

JULY 20

Doing Good

See that no one pays back evil for evil, but always try to do good to each other and to all people.

1 THESSALONIANS 5:15 NLT

We get to choose our response when others harm us. The more we get our fuel and validation from the presence of the Lord, the more gracious, peaceful, and loving we are able to be. If we are secure in God's love, we are less likely to be offended and spiteful when people wrong us.

Today is a fresh opportunity to treat others with dignity, honor, and kindness. Building a habit of mindfulness toward others takes practice and intention. It also happens as we fill up on the love of God. Let's be sure to spend time in his presence receiving what he so willingly offers. Doing good starts with knowing the source of all good things.

Good Father, fill me up with mercy and kindness today as I turn my attention toward you again. Show me the way of peace and goodness, and I will walk in it.

JULY 21

Our Healing

He was pierced for our transgressions, he was crushed for our iniquities; the punishment that brought us peace was on him, and by his wounds we are healed.

Isaiah 53:5 NIV

Christ is our healing, our hope, and our peace. Everything we need and long for is found in him. With love he suffered to pay for the freedom of our souls. Everything he did in life and death was motivated by a desire to love us and do the will of God.

Jesus has removed every barrier that could stand in the way of perfect love. He endured the unthinkable so we would be set free. By his wounds we are healed. Our minds, hearts, and bodies are made right because of what Jesus has done. We owe him everything because without him we would be crushed under the impossible burden of sin and death.

Lord Jesus, thank you for the healing I have in you. Tend to the wounds in my heart and bring greater wholeness to my being. I am yours.

JULY 22

Sweet Wisdom

*My son, eat honey, for it is good,
and the drippings of the honeycomb are sweet to your taste.
Know that wisdom is such to your soul;
if you find it, there will be a future,
and your hope will not be cut off.*

PROVERBS 24:13-14 ESV

The sweetness of wisdom is revealed as we walk it out. Wisdom will never lead us astray. Though we may encounter resistance from others, God's ways are always best. His wisdom provides an open pathway to his kingdom where there is no corruption, manipulation, or fear.

Wisdom offers us a future and hope that will not be cut off. Why would we lean on our own understanding when God offers us the wisdom of his ways? They are for our good and his glory. His wisdom is sweet to the taste and satisfying to the soul. There is life, peace, and rest in choosing God's wise ways over the ways of this world.

God, you are the author of every good and perfect thing. You are the source of truth and wisdom. I choose to incorporate your wisdom into my choices each and every day.

JULY 23

Alignment Check

*Create in me a pure heart, God,
and make my spirit right again.*

PSALM 51:10 NCV

We all have days when we can't seem to shake off a particular frustration. No matter what we are struggling with, it can feel disheartening to feel like we can't solve the problem we are facing. Whether our emotions feel out of control, or we can't seem to focus on truth, God offers us respite from our internal battles.

When we have hard days, we always have a safe space in Christ. We can go to him with our honest feelings and experiences. When we can't change our own minds or attitudes, the Lord's presence always can. God can set right what has gone awry, and he always knows exactly what we need. He welcomes us with open arms and a heart of understanding.

God, create in me a pure heart, and make my spirit right again. Align me with the truth of your love and bring order to my chaos. Give me peace in your presence as I cling to you.

JULY 24

Lit from Within

I pray that the light of God will illuminate the eyes of your imagination, flooding you with light, until you experience the full revelation of the hope of his calling—that is, the wealth of God's glorious inheritances that he finds in us, his holy ones!

EPHESIANS 1:18 TPT

The light of God's love is powerful. It can expand our imaginations, flooding us with creativity, goodness, and pure joy. There is power in his presence, and there is always more revelation available. The Spirit is ready to increase our knowledge of the Lord whenever we ask.

Read today's verse again. Pray it over your own heart and mind. As you declare Scripture over yourself, God meets you with his revelatory wisdom. May you know the power of his presence as it wraps around you. You are the glorious inheritance of Christ. He delights in you!

Holy One, open my eyes and increase my awareness of your life-giving truth. I am yours, and you are mine. What a beautiful reality.

JULY 25

Reliable Leader

*"I will instruct you and teach you
in the way which you should go;
I will advise you with My eye upon you."*

Psalm 32:8 NASB

When we accept God's leadership, we experience comfort and relief. The realization that we don't have to be in control allows us to rest, relax, and worship with abandon. God has everything handled. We are the recipients of his expert care and guidance. Instead of micromanaging and worrying, we can loosen our grasp and acknowledge his authority.

You don't have to figure everything out on your own. God leads you as you look to him. His eternal perspective means he is a much better pilot than you are. You can trust his ability to lead you where you need to be. He knows what is best, and he knows every single step you need to take. Lay down your desire for control and experience the rest found in surrendering to his plans.

God, you are the one I rely on through every season of life. I trust that you are never thrown off by the unexpected. Fill me with confidence as I follow you.

JULY 26

Great Understanding

*The entrance of Your words gives light;
It gives understanding to the simple.*

Psalm 119:130 NKJV

There is no problem God cannot solve. There is no challenge he cannot overcome. When we come up against roadblocks in life, we can depend on his ability to lead us through or around them. His plans never fail, and he knows the solution to every problem.

When God speaks, he gives clarity to confusion. Whether our problems are big or small, we can trust him to help us with each one. As we submit our lives to him, he gives us his perspective and encourages us with his Word. He settles our anxieties and illuminates the darkest parts of our lives with his presence.

God, thank you for the power of your Word that breaks through walls of confusion and brings understanding and peace. Speak freely throughout my day. My ears are turned toward your voice.

JULY 27

Just Ask

If any of you lacks wisdom, he should ask God—who gives to all generously and ungrudgingly—and it will be given to him.

JAMES 1:5 CSB

God's ears are open at all times. He is always listening for those who call on him. There are no busy signals or waiting lines. He is able to hear us at any time, in any place, and at any volume. We can freely ask him for whatever we need.

God is quick to give wisdom to everyone who asks. His wisdom opens doors and creates solutions. He offers practical steps when you are stuck in indecision. It reveals his nature, for it will never suggest anything that opposes him. Eagerly ask for wisdom with the expectation that God will give it to you. Don't hesitate, for he is generous and ready to act.

Generous One, thank you for the power of your wisdom. Thank you for readily offering it to me at all times. When I am struggling, remind me that all I need to do is ask for your help.

JULY 28

Cheerful Choices

You must each decide in your heart how much to give. And don't give reluctantly or in response to pressure. "For God loves a person who gives cheerfully."

2 Corinthians 9:7 NLT

When we partner with God by being generous, there is joy to feast on. The best part about being generous according to God's standards is that there isn't a precise formula we must follow. He doesn't require us to give specific things or particular amounts of money. His higher standard is that we give with a cheerful heart. He doesn't want us to give for the sake of giving.

Examine your heart today. What do you have to give? As God reveals opportunities to be generous, respond by adhering to his standard rather than your own. Give freely with a cheerful heart and without obligation. When you take ownership over your generosity, you align yourself with God's plans.

Joyful God, help me grow in generosity. Teach me how to give with a cheerful heart instead of obligation. Show me opportunities to express your kindness and love to others.

JULY 29

Solid Steps

Whether you turn to the right or to the left, your ears will hear a voice behind you, saying, "This is the way; walk in it."

Isaiah 30:21 NIV

Quiet confidence is ours as we rely on the faithful leadership of God. We cannot know every step of the path ahead or the twists and turns that will come. However, we can trust that God will be with us along the way. He actively guides us as we rely on him.

When you are stuck in indecision, invite the voice of God to break through the noise. His voice, like a whisper in your ear, will direct your steps. As you go about your day, give God authority to lead you where he wants you to go. Submit yourself to his ways and trust the peace that comes with his presence.

Father, I trust your guidance. I cannot escape your presence, and for that I am grateful. I need you with me every step of the way. Give me grace to follow you closely.

JULY 30

Give and Receive

"Give and it will be given to you. Good measure, pressed down, shaken together, running over, will be put into your lap. For with the measure you use it will be measured back to you."

Luke 6:38 ESV

The principle of generosity is a godly one. Scripture teaches that when we give, God returns the blessing back to us. Generosity benefits others and ourselves. Giving to others with a cheerful heart makes room in our lives to receive. There is no need to withhold our time, possessions, or resources because God is always capable of providing more.

For some people it seems easy to give freely and generously. In contrast, other people refuse to give and consistently complain that they don't have enough. Who do you think has a lighter heart? Generosity leads to joy while a scarcity mindset leads to dissatisfaction and selfishness. Join your heart with God's and operate with compassion and generosity.

Generous Father, I don't want fear to keep me from growing in generosity. You are able to provide, and I trust you to be faithful. I will gladly join you in giving to others.

JULY 31

Under His Protection

> Those who go to God Most High for safety
> will be protected by the Almighty.
> I will say to the Lord, "You are my place of
> safety and protection.
> You are my God and I trust you."
>
> PSALM 91:1-2 NCV

There is no safer place than God's presence. We don't have to fly around the world to find refuge. We turn our desperate hearts to the Lord, and we come under his protection right then and there. His ability to meet our needs is unlimited.

When your heart wavers, turn to God. When your soul is shaking, run to the Lord Most High. He is able to cover you and comfort you. He will be your place of safety and protection. He is worthy of your trust, for he is faithful, kind, and true. There is absolutely nothing that he cannot help you through!

Powerful Protector, be my defender when I feel exposed. Keep watch over me and settle my anxious heart. Give me peace in your presence. I trust you to protect me.

August

Cast your cares on the Lord
and he will sustain you;
he will never let
the righteous be shaken.

PSALM 55:22 NIV

AUGUST 1

Consistency Pays Off

"I know all that you've done for me—your love and faith, your ministry and steadfast perseverance. In fact, you now excel in these virtues even more than at the first."

REVELATION 2:19 TPT

We go from glory to glory in Christ. As we follow him and apply his law of love to our lives, we grow in grace. When we trust him through the hills and valleys of this life, we will consistently experience his love, wisdom, and companionship. Walking hand in hand with him gives us perseverance and strength.

Each day is an opportunity to stay the course. Life is not linear, and it won't look the same through each stage and season. The only thing that remains the same is the character of God and the sacrificial love of Jesus. As we trust the Lord through the changes of this life, we will continue to grow in love, kindness, peace, and compassion.

Savior, thank you for the example you set. Thank you for the comfort, strength, and companionship you offer through the Spirit. I choose to stay on your path of love.

AUGUST 2

Eternal Glory

Our momentary, light affliction is producing for us an eternal weight of glory far beyond all comparison, while we look not at the things which are seen, but at the things which are not seen; for the things which are seen are temporal, but the things which are not seen are eternal.

2 Corinthians 4:17-18 NASB

Suffering is only temporary. It will not last forever. As we continue to cling to Christ through the ups and downs of life, we will know the relief of his presence, the comfort of his love, and the power of his resurrection life.

There is more at work than we can see, and the glory of God's kingdom is beyond our comprehension. It is more beautiful than we can imagine, and it will exceed our greatest expectations. As we wait, we get glimpses of this glory in the fellowship of God's Spirit. No matter what today looks like, there is hope for tomorrow.

Glorious One, there is no one like you in all the earth. Give me a glimpse of your glory today. Fill me with anticipation for the perfection of your kingdom.

AUGUST 3

Countless Reasons

> I will hope continually,
> And will praise You yet more and more.
>
> PSALM 71:14 NKJV

The more life we live the more opportunities we have to experience the goodness of God. Wherever we are, there is the joy of his presence. No matter how we feel, there is something to be thankful for. In all things we can off God our worship and praise. We can open our hearts to him and expect him to bless us with his presence.

As you continue to put your hope in the Lord, don't forget to praise him. Intentionally notice the bits of beauty in your life and use them as an opportunity to worship God. There are countless reasons to praise him. Gratitude is like a muscle, and the more you use it the stronger it will become.

Gracious God, my hope is in your faithfulness. Give me grace to praise you more with each passing day. Give me eyes to see the beauty you put in my life.

AUGUST 4

Unbothered

"When you pass through the waters,
I will be with you,
and the rivers will not overwhelm you.
When you walk through the fire,
you will not be scorched,
and the flame will not burn you."

ISAIAH 43:2 CSB

It is no small thing to go through a flood. It's not minor to walk through fire. These are terrifying situations, yet the Lord promises to be with us in our trials and troubles no matter how fierce they are. His presence is constant, and it covers us completely.

God's love is powerful, and his peace passes all understanding. No matter the strength of the storms we experience, God's presence is persistent. It will never give up or let us go. This is our great hope and our gracious assurance. When we are surrendered to him, God's love does not lift from our lives.

Lord, I am grateful to know the confident assurance of your presence. Thank you for being with me through the storms of life. Surround me with your presence and fill me with peace.

AUGUST 5

Bold Approach

Let us come boldly to the throne of our gracious God. There we will receive his mercy, and we will find grace to help us when we need it most.

HEBREWS 4:16 NLT

We don't need to keep the Lord at a distance. There is no reason to hold back when he longs for us to be close to him. Even on our worst days, God will not turn us away. As dearly loved children we can approach his throne of grace with boldness.

Go to God no matter how long it has been since you have. You will find that his character is steadfast and unchanging. His loyal love cannot be interrupted by anything including your own choices and struggles. His grace and mercy are available when you need them most.

Gracious God, I come boldly before your throne today. You are my God, and I need your grace. Give me confidence to run to you without hesitation or shame.

AUGUST 6

Ask Seek Knock

"Ask and it will be given to you; seek and you will find; knock and the door will be opened to you."

Luke 11:13 NIV

When we ask for wisdom, we receive it. When we ask for help, it is ours. There aren't closed doors in God's kingdom. He is eager to offer us help when we need it. Our own weaknesses and limitations are simply opportunities to humbly receive the abundance God offers.

When we come up against roadblocks or closed doors, we don't need to immediately turn away. We can prayerfully knock and allow God to give us wisdom. He might lead us through it, or he might show us another path. There is power in trusting his leadership with a humble heart.

Lord, thank you for the reminder that we are all lacking in some way or another. Give me a growth mindset and the humility to admit when I need help. Thank you for your promised guidance and provision.

AUGUST 7

Quick Returns

*On the day I called, you answered me;
my strength of soul you increased.*

PSALM 138:3 ESV

God is always ready and willing to help. Not every answer is immediate, but the power of his presence is. He hears us when we call on him, and he strengthens our weary souls. He sees exactly what we need, and he provides for us when we trust him.

There are some needs that have to be addressed immediately. In other situations, you can take extra time to work something out. You use your judgment to gauge what is needed. God does the same thing, but you can expect perfection from him. His timing is ideal, and the solutions he offers are always exactly what is needed. He knows what to do in every circumstance.

Faithful Father, thank you for answering me when I call on you. I will not hesitate to reach out to you throughout the day. You are my help, and I rely on your Spirit to strengthen me.

AUGUST 8

Aroma of Love

Live a life of love just as Christ loved us and gave himself for us as a sweet-smelling offering and sacrifice to God.

EPHESIANS 5:2 NCV

Jesus revealed the power of God's love throughout his ministry of healing and deliverance. He painted a picture of God's mercy through his sacrifice and resurrection. He endured great suffering so we could tangibly experience God's love and desire for relationship with us.

Loving others is a sweet-smelling offering to God. Displaying his character to the world around you is an act of worship. As you lay your life down for your friends and neighbors, you lay your life down for God. Choosing love over self-preservation hurts, but it is always worth it. He sees every act of sacrifice and service. He is honored by the love in your life.

Jesus, you are worthy of my praise and devotion. You are worthy of every sacrifice I make. Your love fuels mine. It is an honor to offer my life in your name.

AUGUST 9

Timely Encouragement

*Yahweh, you have heard the desires of the humble
and seen their hopes.
You will hear their cries and encourage their hearts.*

Psalm 10:17 tpt

God doesn't encourage us with blanket statements or vague truths. He speaks into each circumstance with sharp wisdom and complete compassion. Our hearts are encouraged because the Lord always knows exactly what we need to hear, experience, and receive in each unique moment.

God's encouragement isn't limited to times of suffering or pain. He also speaks life into your hopes and desires. He affirms you when you do the right thing, and he gives you confidence and boldness to pursue his life-giving will. He is beside you cheering you on in seasons of joy, and he is ready to comfort you when you are hurting.

Father, thank you for being present throughout every season. Thank you for holding all my emotions with gentleness and wisdom. Encourage me today and give me courage to pursue your will.

AUGUST 10

In Spirit and Truth

"God is spirit, and those who worship Him must worship in spirit and truth."

JOHN 4:24 NASB

To worship the Lord in spirit and truth is to be connected to him through our yielded hearts. When we acknowledge his lordship, we gain uninterrupted fellowship with his Spirit. We know him, and we are known by him. We offer each day, breath, and action to him with the humble realization that he is the source of everything good in our lives.

Your worship of God comes from the deep soul connection between you and him. The highest form of praise is the offering of a humble and contrite heart. When you willingly align your heart with him, you are actively living out his greatest desire for your life. Being one with him is your greatest pursuit and his greatest joy.

Lord, I want to worship you in spirit and truth. Align my heart with yours and keep my eyes fixed on you. You are all I want and all I need. May my thoughts and actions be honoring to you.

AUGUST 11

Bathed in Mercy

Let Your mercy, O Lord, be upon us,
Just as we hope in You.

Psalm 33:22 nkjv

When we turn our faces to the sun, we soak in the heat of its rays. When we set our hope on the Lord, it has the same effect on our hearts. Like sunflowers turning toward the sun, we turn toward the Lord and experience the life-giving light of his love.

The light of God's mercy doesn't fade even when night falls. Our hope is sure when it is set on the Lord. He who is unchanging and powerful to save will never let us down. We find rest in his presence, and we find peace in his comforting nearness. We are never without it whether we sense it or not. He is all we need and so much more.

Lord, let the light of your mercy shine on me. My hope is in you, and I won't be disappointed. Help me keep my eyes on you for all my days.

AUGUST 12

Look Up

*Lord, your faithful love reaches to heaven,
your faithfulness to the clouds.*

Psalm 36:5 csb

Worry can cloud our vision and alter our perspective. It causes us to forget the truth and focus on imaginary scenarios. When we focus on worry, we lose sight of God's faithfulness. He has taken care of us in the past, and he will continue to do so. There is no limit to his love. It reaches far beyond anything we can see.

The faithfulness of God never diminishes no matter how we feel about it. Let's take time to rest in God's present goodness by going outside and looking up to the sky. The same God who created the heavens longs to remind us of his provision and care.

Faithful One, I need to be reminded of your wisdom and faithfulness. Thank you for displaying your glory in the sky. Your love extends to the heavens and beyond.

AUGUST 13

Valuables

"Wherever your treasure is, there the desires of your heart will also be."

MATTHEW 6:21 NLT

We give our attention and energy to whatever we value most. If we value what others think of us, we will do all we can to present ourselves at our best. If we value money, we will look for ways to make as much as we can. These treasures are fleeting, and the search for them is fruitless.

The values of God's kingdom are lasting. We can never run out of his love. Our hearts follow what we truly value, but we don't need to be discouraged if our priorities aren't quite right. God is capable of changing our hearts. If our desire is to follow him, he will give us grace to keep our gaze on him.

Holy One, I am grateful that it's never too late to shift my course. May your values become more important to me than the fleeting treasures of this world.

AUGUST 14

Refreshing Returns

> A generous person will prosper;
> whoever refreshes others will be refreshed.
>
> PROVERBS 11:25 NIV

In God's kingdom we often get what we give. God asks us to live according to his character, but he also promises it will be reciprocated. He doesn't leave his children empty handed. He is gracious and generous toward us when our lives align with his values. We receive grace upon grace from God, so why would we withhold what we've been freely given?

When we move in mercy, kindness, generosity, and encouragement, we reflect the likeness of our heavenly Father. We don't have to be stingy with our love. In God's kingdom it is an unlimited resource. We can bless others with the confident expectation that God will also bless us.

Gracious Father, I choose to move in generosity and encouragement knowing I will receive it back. Your gracious provision gives me confidence to lay my life down for others.

AUGUST 15

Under His Wings

*He will deliver you from the snare of the fowler
and from the deadly pestilence.
He will cover you with his pinions,
and under his wings you will find refuge.*

PSALM 91:3-4 ESV

The presence of God is a shield. We can take refuge under his wings anytime and anywhere. He delivers us from fear and covers us with his protective love. His presence is our peace no matter what our circumstances look like. He keeps our feet steady even when the world is shaking.

When anxiety heightens, we can run to the shelter of the Most High. We can find rest in his confident care. There is no storm or battle that can keep us from the love of God. He is a safe place for his people to land, and he hems us in with his faithfulness.

Most High, you are my safe place, and I run into the shelter of your presence today. Cover me and settle my heart. Please give me rest, peace, and the strength I need to go on.

AUGUST 16

Pleasing Sacrifices

Do not forget to do good to others, and share with them, because such sacrifices please God.

Hebrews 13:16 NCV

God is not difficult to please. When we love others, he is proud of how we represent him. He is delighted by our attempts to share his character with others. We honor him by doing good, being generous with what we have, and caring for those who are vulnerable.

We don't earn God's love by doing the right thing, but that doesn't mean he isn't proud of us. He is pleased when we make sacrifices for people who need it. He delights in our growth, and he is aware of our efforts. Doing God's work because it makes him happy is not the same thing as doing it to gain salvation or approval.

Father, thank you for opportunities to grow in generosity, grace, and goodness. Teach me how to love others like you do. I want my thoughts, words, and actions to be pleasing to you.

AUGUST 17

Empowering Love

Love empowers us to fulfill the law of the Anointed One as we carry each other's troubles.

GALATIANS 6:2 TPT

Love empowers us to support one another, and it also empowers us to please God. When we feel like we have nothing left to give, God's love gives us strength. He provides what we need to be kind, compassionate, and servant-hearted toward others.

We were not made to navigate life alone. We all struggle and suffer, and we shouldn't bear that weight on our own. We were made to carry each other's troubles. Everyone's burdens are lighter when the weight is shared. It is pleasing to God when we notice each other's pain and serve each other in genuine ways.

Lord, your love strengthens my heart and gives me the motivation to keep going. Show me opportunities to lighten the load of those around me. May I love others in the same way you love me.

AUGUST 18

Always Enough

God will generously provide all you need. Then you will always have everything you need and plenty left over to share with others.

2 Corinthians 9:8 NLT

God has fully equipped each of us. He provides for us in a multitude of ways. By his grace we are able to live in a way that pleases him. Our own efforts don't amount to much, but his grace gives us strength for every good deed. It never runs out and it is always accessible.

God's abundant grace ensures we have exactly what we need. Every challenge and problem are overcome by his strength. As he provides for us, we share with others. We can be gracious toward others because he is so gracious with us. We can spread his love to everyone we come in contact with because he has filled us to overflowing.

Generous One, thank you for your sufficient grace that not only meets my needs but provides me with extra to offer others. Show me opportunities to be compassionate, generous, and gracious toward others.

AUGUST 19

Bound in Love

Above all these things put on love, which is the bond of perfection.

Colossians 3:14 NKJV

There are many things that connect us to one another. Shared interests, hobbies, and beliefs pull us toward like-minded people. However, nothing bonds us more deeply to one another than love. This is why Scripture says to put on love above all things.

It is no small thing to love to others. Though our interests or opinions may change with time, love isn't something to be lost along the way. It only grows stronger and deeper with time. As we are filled by God's love, we can offer it without hesitation. He has provided us with a limitless well to draw from. When loving others is our priority, we can be confident God will help us.

Loving Lord, thank you for the power of love's connection. Teach me how to love like you do. Soften my heart and give me grace to lay my life down for others.

AUGUST 20

Character on Display

A noble person plans noble things;
he stands up for noble causes.

ISAIAH 32:8 CSB

Our lives reveal the values we hold. We can't hide our true intentions for long. Eventually, the attitude of our hearts will be on full display because our character is embodied by our actions. Noble people plan noble things, while corrupt people are revealed by the wake of chaos they leave behind.

Our actions matter. It is not enough to say we believe something but never act on it. Our true beliefs play out in our choices whether we are aware of them or not. If there are discrepancies in our hearts, God can lift us from pits of our own making and set us on the solid foundation of his love. It is never too late to make better choices or align our heart with God.

Savior, I trust your judgment. Show me if there is any part of my character that doesn't align with yours. Give me grace to change the way I act.

AUGUST 21

Heavenly Insight

I pray for you constantly, asking God, the glorious Father of our Lord Jesus Christ, to give you spiritual wisdom and insight so that you might grow in your knowledge of God.

EPHESIANS 1:17 NLT

Each day is an opportunity for growth. We are not stuck or limited by the way we currently think. We can change our minds, and we can approach problems from a different angle. We can embrace humility and admit that we don't know everything. It is healthy to be open to growth and change.

There is spiritual wisdom and insight available today. Ask the Holy Spirit to teach you the ways of God. Ask for specific steps to grow in your knowledge of him. There is always more to discover in the glorious reality of God's presence. Don't remain stagnant when you could be embracing an exciting journey of faith.

Holy Spirit, I am your vessel, and I am open to you today. I admit there is so much I do not know. Increase my understanding and give me heavenly insight.

AUGUST 22

Undying Hope

This truth gives them confidence that they have eternal life, which God—who does not lie—promised them before the world began. And now at just the right time he has revealed this message, which we announce to everyone. It is by the command of God our Savior that I have been entrusted with this work for him.

TITUS 1:2-3 NLT

God's promises never expire. It doesn't matter how long they take to come to fruition; he is never late. Though God's timing is different than ours, we must recognize his sovereignty and perfection. If God has orchestrated something, who are we to question it? We can rest in his ability to weave all of history together.

God's greatest promise is our eternal hope. Jesus is the fulfillment of that hope. In Christ, we come to the Father and experience liberation from sin and death. We are confident that we will have eternal life because through Christ God has already proven himself faithful. We don't have anything to worry about.

Eternal One, thank you for fulfilling your promises through Jesus. Fill me with confidence that you will continue to be faithful. In you I have eternal security.

AUGUST 23

Justified by Faith

We know that a person is not justified by works of the law but through faith in Jesus Christ, so we also have believed in Christ Jesus, in order to be justified by faith in Christ and not by works of the law, because by works of the law no one will be justified.

GALATIANS 2:16 ESV

No one is justified by the works of the law because no one can keep them perfectly. We all fall short of the glory of God. It is only through the saving grace of Jesus that we experience justification and freedom from sin, death, fear, and shame.

You can only be justified by faith which leads you to rely on Jesus. There is so much freedom in realizing that there is nothing you can do to earn God's favor. He is not impressed by your work, nor is he discouraged by your weakness. There is no way you can bear the burden of your sin or meet God's standard of perfection. Jesus' death and resurrection is an invitation for you to let go and rest in the work he has already done.

Christ Jesus, my faith is in you. Your presence is where I find rest and peace of mind. Keep me from putting too much weight on the work that I do.

AUGUST 24

Even an Inkling

"The Father is the One who sent me. No one can come to me unless the Father draws him to me, and I will raise that person up on the last day."

John 6:44 NCV

All who come to Jesus are ultimately drawn by the hand of the Father. God can work with the smallest inkling of curiosity toward him. He can soften hardened hearts, and he can expand a mustard seed of faith. We are saved by his grace rather than our strength or ability.

God's work in our lives gives us confidence and security. It doesn't matter how small our faith seems; God can work miracles with it. Take hope in the smallest seeds of faith in your heart, and let it move you toward Jesus today. He can do mighty things with the tiniest offering.

Lord Jesus, thank you for the seeds of faith you have planted in my heart. Draw me close to you and increase my faith. Thank you for your grace and mercy.

AUGUST 25

Great God

"Yet through you everyone will know who I really am. Those from the rising sun in the east to the west, everyone everywhere will know that I am Yahweh, the one and only God, and there is no other."

ISAIAH 45:6 TPT

As followers of God, we want the nations to know his name. We want to do God's work, yet there is relief in knowing God doesn't need us. He chooses us, and he loves us. He longs to partner with us, but he could surely do the work on his own. He uses our weaknesses and humanity to share his sacrificial love.

Take the pressure off yourself. God's work is not meant to be a burden. He does not want you to burn out or work yourself toward bitterness and cynicism. He wants to advance his kingdom by working with you. He does not require too much, and he is constantly aware of your weaknesses. If you are struggling, it might be because you are striving on your own rather than partnering with him in grace.

Lord, I am humbled to be used for your purposes. Strengthen me where I am weak and help me declare your name wherever I go. May my life reveal your love to others.

AUGUST 26

Righteous Faith

> "Now look toward the heavens and count the stars, if you are able to count them…. So shall your descendants be." Then he believed in the LORD; and He credited it to him as righteousness.
>
> GENESIS 15:5-6 NASB

Take a look at the promise God made to Abraham in today's verse. It sounded too good to be true. It wasn't a prophecy of doom or a threat to stay in line. It was a powerful promise that God would make his family outstandingly fruitful.

Consider the reality of Abraham's life in light of God's promise. He was an old man before he had Isaac, but God was faithful to his word. Through both Ishmael and Isaac, Abraham's descendants are many. Abraham believed God, and it was credited to him as righteousness. When we take God at his Word, even when it seems too good to be true, he does the same with us.

Faithful God, I am encouraged by the faith of those who have gone before me. I am astounded by your faithfulness to every generation. Strengthen my faith and help me hold fast to your promises.

AUGUST 27

The Same Jesus

Jesus Christ is the same yesterday, today, and forever.

HEBREWS 13:8 NKJV

What a comfort it is to know that Jesus is the same mercifully kind Savior he always has been. He is the same healer, wise teacher, and friend as was displayed in the Bible. He has the power to bring the dead to life and to lead us into the glory of eternity.

When you read Scripture, what stands out to you about Jesus? What do you love about him? He is the same now as he was then. There is nothing you can read about him that isn't possible today. He is alive, and he hasn't changed. You can know him in Spirit and in truth as the Holy Spirit reveals his nature to you in ever-expanding ways.

Merciful Jesus, I am in awe of who you are. Your beautiful kindness, powerful wisdom, and healing touch are all glimpses of your perfection. Meet me today through the fellowship of the Spirit and minister to my heart.

AUGUST 28

Promise Keeper

By faith even Sarah herself, when she was unable to have children, received power to conceive offspring, even though she was past the age, since she considered that the one who had promised was faithful.

Hebrews 11:11 csb

Do you remember Sarah's reaction to the news that she would have a child in her old age? She laughed. She was astounded by the suggestion that her tired body could create life. It seemed too good to be true. Nothing is impossible with the Lord, and he is faithful even when his promises cause us to laugh.

If you had been in Sarah's shoes, would you have reacted differently? You would probably have been just as surprised by what was said to you. God was faithful to Sarah despite her shock, and he will be faithful to you now even if you doubt him sometimes. Instead of being discouraged by your reactions, be encouraged by his reliability.

Father, you are faithful even when I falter. Lift my eyes toward you and give me a greater measure of resolve. Give me confidence to believe what you say.

AUGUST 29

Jesus Understands

This High Priest of ours understands our weaknesses, for he faced all of the same testings we do, yet he did not sin.

Hebrews 4:15 NLT

Though Jesus is the Son of God, he is also the Son of Man. While he walked the earth, he experienced the full spectrum of human emotions. He knew what it was like to struggle and grow. He knew hunger and exhaustion. He experienced the limits of his frail humanity, yet he was perfect and without sin.

We can take hope in the fellowship of Christ. He understands all of our struggles, and he is acquainted with our suffering. He knows our weaknesses, and we can trust him to help us with each one. He is approachable and kind no matter how we are received or rejected by others. He will never turn us away when we come to him.

Lord Jesus, I know you understand my life and my struggles. You know what it feels like to grieve and be misunderstood. You are my great High Priest, and I will come to you with all my weaknesses.

AUGUST 30

Spiritual Renewal

He saved us, not because of righteous things we had done, but because of his mercy. He saved us through the washing of rebirth and renewal by the Holy Spirit.

TITUS 3:5 NIV

Not only do we experience the salvation of our souls in Christ, but we also receive rebirth and renewal in his Spirit. Spiritual renewal is something we can experience over and over again. There is no need to become stagnant in our faith, for there is always something new to experience in God's great mercy.

God is relational. He doesn't apply formulas to our lives. He isn't out of touch or out of reach. He treats us with compassion and love, and he offers exactly what we need each day. His mercy is vast, but it is not generic. He cares for us specifically and with intention. Though it may remain a mystery as to how he does it, his precise love is gift.

God, thank you for how powerfully you minister to each of us. Thank you for how precisely you minister to me! Bring greater renewal to my own spirit today.

AUGUST 31

Walk by Faith

We walk by faith, not by sight.

2 Corinthians 5:7 esv

If we were to rely on our physical senses alone there would be numerous reasons to give into fear. There would be a plethora of limitations that we could not see beyond. We would consistently come up against barriers and closed doors. Faith is necessary to follow Jesus. We must be able to see with the eyes of our hearts.

When we walk by faith, we rely on the leadership of God's love in every stage of life. He is never at a loss for what to do. He is full of reliable strength and wisdom that brings breakthroughs. When we don't know how to move, the answer is not to give up. The answer is to lean into the Lord. We ask for his help, and he shows us the way forward as we trust him.

Lord, I walk by faith not by sight. Sight can only get me so far, but faith moves mountains. I'm so grateful for your leadership and your faithfulness.

September

May the favor of the Lord our God rest on us;
establish the work of our hands for us—
yes, establish the work of our hands.

PSALM 90:17 NIV

SEPTEMBER 1

First and Last

"This is what the Lord says—
Israel's King and Redeemer, the Lord Almighty:
I am the first and I am the last;
apart from me there is no God."

ISAIAH 44:6 NIV

No one comes before and no one will come after the Lord Almighty. He is the King of all the earth and our great Redeemer. Though God is eternal, he was at the beginning of the earth, and he will be at its end.

May our fears be relieved in the unrelenting presence and power of God our Creator. He is able to do all things, and he does them well. We can trust him with our cares and troubles. He isn't far away. He was present at the beginning of all things, and he'll be at the end. He's present in every moment in between as well.

Lord, may I never forget how relentless your love is. I'm so grateful to lean on you and your great wisdom, power, and grace.

SEPTEMBER 2

What You Know

*I know, Lord, that you are for me,
and I will never fear what man can do to me.
For you stand beside me as my hero who rescues me.*

PSALM 118:6-7 TPT

Our beliefs dictate how we move in the world. If we are confident of God's love leading us in this life, we have nothing to fear. If we live in the shadow of his mercy, why would we be anxious? God is our rescuer, and he is also defender of the weak.

Are you sure of God's heart for you? He loves you. Even when he corrects you, he is doing what is best for you. He knows your strengths and weaknesses, and he knows what you are capable of. He knows what the best version of you looks like, and he equips you to become it. He lifts you up from the mire and sets your feet on solid ground.

Lord, when you move, I see your kindness at work. Show me today how your heart is for me and reveal how I can stand on your faithfulness.

SEPTEMBER 3

No Weapon

*"No weapon that is formed against you will succeed;
And you will condemn every tongue
that accuses you in judgment.
This is the heritage of the servants of the Lord,
And their vindication is from Me," declares the Lord.*

ISAIAH 54:17 NASB

The Lord is beautiful in all his ways. He does not overlook the vulnerable or oppressed. He promises to be close to the brokenhearted and comfort those who mourn. He is powerful to save all who call upon his name. As we find refuge in him, he provides protection and safety.

What confidence we have in God's faithfulness. When we walk in the light of God's ways, there is nothing to fear. Our God is for us. He promises to stay with us until we arrive before him in the age to come. There is heartfelt rest and respite from worry for all who trust in him.

Lord, you are my peace and my strength. I rely on your faithfulness, and I trust your plans. Come closer today and wrap me in your love.

SEPTEMBER 4

Prayerful Perseverance

Pray in the Spirit at all times and on every occasion. Stay alert and be persistent in your prayers for all believers everywhere.

EPHESIANS 6:18 NLT

As we live under the gaze of our good Father, we have no reason to fear. We can remain steady even when our circumstances are overwhelming. Prayer keeps our awareness fixed on God who never leaves us. Prayer points our hearts toward our Savior, for with him nothing is impossible.

A prayerful lifestyle is fruit of being surrendered to God. We keep our hearts and hands open to his leadership and mercy. We follow where he leads. We present him with our heartfelt prayers, and he relieves our worries and gives us wisdom. He is reliable and worthy of our dependence.

Lord, you have my heart. Give me perseverance in prayer and help me hear your voice correctly. I am open to your corrections and am willing to follow you.

SEPTEMBER 5

Focused Gaze

*Let your eyes look forward;
fix your gaze straight ahead.
Carefully consider the path for your feet,
and all your ways will be established.*

PROVERBS 4:25-26 CSB

Sometimes being faithful means taking a few steps and seeing whether the path is secure or not. We won't always see the entire road clearly. This doesn't mean that we shouldn't step out. Instead, we are called to trust God with each solitary movement. He knows where he is taking us, and we get to walk hand-in-hand the whole way.

A focused gaze is not sidetracked by distractions. It keeps the vision in view. Sometimes we need to remove the distractions around us, and other times we simply need to put our attention where it belongs. May we look to the Lord no matter what is going on around us. No matter what comes and goes, he remains. If we shift our gaze toward him, we will see that he is always in view.

Lord Jesus, I fix my gaze on you. Give me grace to steady despite distractions. You are my faithful leader and friend. I focus my attention on you alone.

SEPTEMBER 6

Grounded Trust

Don't love money; be satisfied with what you have. For God has said, "I will never fail you. I will never abandon you."

HEBREWS 13:5 NLT

Money comes and goes. Its value varies and changes with the economy. When we put our trust in money, we will always be disappointed. When we are constantly wanting more, we will never be satisfied. This is why we are encouraged to be happy with what we have. Satisfaction breeds contentment, and it allows us to focus on what truly matters.

God doesn't want us to worry about money. His promise to never fail rings true when we are tempted to give in to anxiety. His kingdom is full of wisdom about how to manage our finances and how to trust him for provision. In all things, he is faithful.

Provider, I don't want to be on an endless quest for more. Help me enjoy what you've already given me while trusting you to provide what I need. You are so good to me, and I trust you.

We Are His

> Know that the Lord is God.
> It is he who made us, and we are his;
> we are his people, the sheep of his pasture.
>
> PSALM 100:3 NIV

As believers, we don't have to question who we are. Identity is so important. When we struggle to know where we belong, we may feel as if we are floundering. We were lovingly created with purpose and intention. There is no greater purpose than to know God and be known by him. He is the Creator, and we belong to him.

We are part of God's family. He is our Shepherd, and we are his flock. He lovingly cares for us and faithfully watches over us. He protects us from the enemy who would steal, kill, and destroy. He shares all that is his, and we can rest in the love of his presence. He is our faithful Father and constant friend who never leaves us.

Lord, thank you for being my caring Shepherd. I trust you to guide me and protect me. Give me eyes to see and ears to hear your voice.

SEPTEMBER 8

Stand and Shine

Arise, shine, for your light has come, and the glory of the Lord has risen upon you.

ISAIAH 60:1 ESV

God invites each of us to be fully satisfied in his presence. Knowing him and being known by him is our highest purpose and where we find the most satisfaction. As his creation, our souls are intertwined with his. We are most at home when we allow the light of his love to shine on our lives.

It can be refreshing to focus on being rather than doing. Stand in the light of God's love and soak it in. You are made in his image, and you are a reflection of his love. There is nothing more you can do to belong to him. You don't have to try harder. You can stand confidently in the grace of God as it meets you at the cross.

Lord, thank you for your loving-kindness that reaches me no matter where I am. I won't resist it today. I stand in the full light of your mercy, and I won't turn away.

SEPTEMBER 9

Never Lose Hope

Always pray and never lose hope.

LUKE 18:1 NCV

Luke 18 tells the story about a persistent widow who was relentless about going before the judge to plead her case. She just wouldn't give up. This judge was not God-fearing, nor did he care about people. Eventually he was so tired of dealing with the widow that he decided to give her what she asked for just so he would have some peace.

Persistence is powerful. The steady drip of water erodes stone over time. With our own prayerful persistence, we make changes. We may not see progress all at once, but with time the terrain is changed, and we see breakthroughs. Scripture says that God will give his people what is right when they cry out to him day and night. He hears us when we are persistent in prayer.

Lord, thank you for the reminder that persistence and prayer are powerful. I trust you to answer when I call on you. Give me fortitude to persevere even when I don't see progress.

SEPTEMBER 10

His Eye Is on You

> The eyes of the Lord are upon
> even the weakest worshipers who love him—
> those who wait in hope and expectation
> for the strong, steady love of God.
>
> PSALM 33:18 TPT

God does not acknowledge us based on the strength of our faith. His attention isn't given exclusively to those who have it all together. He knows each of his children personally, and his love for each of them is equal. God sees us on our weakest days as clearly as he sees us on our best.

Don't despair when you have a hard day. Take comfort in the powerful presence of your good Father. He sees you in your weakness, and he does not despise your struggles. Instead of doubting his affection for you, wait with the expectation that he will show you his love.

Loving Father, I'm so grateful I don't have to wait until I'm at my best to worship you. I don't have to wait even a second to bring you the prayers of my heart. You are my God, and I trust in you.

SEPTEMBER 11

A Better Way

*Commit your works to the Lord,
And your plans will be established.*

PROVERBS 16:3 NASB

When we commit our work to the Lord, we admit that it's more about him than us. Our hearts stay humble in his presence, and we welcome his leadership even when it takes us to unexpected places. He is a faithful and wise teacher who knows what is best for us. When our work is committed to him, not a moment is wasted.

Have you ever felt like your contributions don't matter? The beautiful thing about the Lord is that even the humblest task brings him glory if it is done in his name. When you work at something with integrity and love, it honors him. As you continually commit your work to him, you become confident that his opinion is the only one that matters.

Faithful One, I commit my day to you. I put my plans in your hands, and I trust you to order them perfectly. May everything I say and do be honoring to you.

SEPTEMBER 12

Ask Anything

"Whatever you ask in My name, that I will do, that the Father may be glorified in the Son. If you ask anything in My name, I will do it."

JOHN 14:13-14 NKJV

Have you ever felt like your questions were a nuisance? Perhaps the person you asked was busy or didn't have time to address you. Even if they had a good reason for being distracted, it hurts to be pushed aside. It's painful to feel like your needs are unimportant. Each of us has an innate need to be noticed, and it stings when we feel overlooked.

God is always aware of you. He invites you to ask anything in his name. He not only hears you, but he moves to answer your prayers. His answers may not look how you want, but that doesn't diminish his acknowledgment of you. You are seen, known, and loved by your Maker. He pays close attention to you, and he longs to be included in the details of your life.

Father, I ask for a greater revelation of your faithful kindness. Thank you for the reminder that I can ask you anything. Give me boldness in prayer and grace to trust your sovereignty.

SEPTEMBER 13

Stillness

He got up, rebuked the wind, and said to the sea, "Silence! Be still!" The wind ceased, and there was a great calm.

MARK 4:39 CSB

God's voice can still surging waves in a moment. He can cause the winds to cease with a single word. If he can manage the raging seas, he can also bring calm to the chaos of our minds and hearts. There is nothing in our lives that is too much for him to handle. He can take the fiercest storms and the most problematic situations and use them for his glory and our good.

Do you trust Jesus to do this for you? You can turn to him when you are afraid just like the disciples did. You can call upon his name and expect him to give you peace when you need it most. He doesn't want you to be violently tossed about by the storms of life. His desire is for you to be secure in his love and confident in his ability to calm the waves.

Lord, I call on your name for peace. Calm my chaos and settle my heart and mind. Give me the quiet confidence that comes from knowing you can do all things.

SEPTEMBER 14

Great Rescuer

The Lord hears his people when they call to him for help. He rescues them from all their troubles.

Psalm 34:17 NLT

When we call to God for help, he hears us. He is not a being far up in the sky. He is not detached from the predicaments of his people. He longs to be close to each of his children. He rescues us from our troubles as we cry out to him.

It doesn't matter how many times you call on the Lord, he is faithful to answer every time. His presence is filled with loyal love. When he responds to you, he does it with kindness, patience, wisdom, and peace. He has all you need and everything you don't know to ask for. May your heart know the confidence of his great love as he rescues you from the troubles you face.

Lord, I won't stop calling out to you for help. Fill me with confidence and an attitude of expectancy. I trust you to answer me when I need it most.

Confident Assurance

Faith is confidence in what we hope for and assurance about what we do not see. This is what the ancients were commended for. By faith we understand that the universe was formed at God's command, so that what is seen was not made out of what was visible.

HEBREWS 11:1-3 NIV

As believers, everything we do relies on our faith in God. Not every act of faith needs to be extraordinary or life changing. Ordinary faith is found as we humbly work with love and integrity. Faith is displayed in the quiet confidence of knowing how we live matters and expecting God to come through for us.

Through fellowship with God's Spirit, we gain assurance and our faith is strengthened. As we spend time with him, we are reminded that he is eternally faithful. We can devote our lives to him knowing we will not be disappointed. God can take our smallest steps of obedience and turn them into something valuable.

Lord, strengthen my faith today. Keep me from scoffing at seemingly insignificant acts of faith. I place my day in your hands, and I trust you to transform it into something that glorifies you.

SEPTEMBER 16

Be Still and Know

*"Be still, and know that I am God.
I will be exalted among the nations,
I will be exalted in the earth!"*

PSALM 46:10 ESV

God is our fortress. He is a place of protection where we can find refuge. When we declare the Lord as our strength, we have no reason to give in to fear. Even if the systems and institutions of the world crumble, our true home is steady. Even if our life doesn't look how we want, our eternal life is secure.

Take time to quiet your heart before the Lord. Take deep breaths and turn your attention toward him. Recall his previous faithfulness and allow him to meet you in the present. God is in the midst of you. He is the one who sustains your life, and he will not let you go. Simply be still and know that he's got you.

God, I quiet myself before you and turn my attention to the nearness of your presence. You are God, and I wait on you.

Keep Reaching

I know that I have not yet reached that goal, but there is one thing I always do. Forgetting the past and straining toward what is ahead, I keep trying to reach the goal and get the prize for which God called me through Christ to the life above.

Philippians 3:13-14 NCV

On some days forward movement is quick and encouraging. On other days it feels as if we aren't getting anywhere. The momentum of our journey isn't the same every day. There are changes to the pace, and that's to be expected. We don't have to be discouraged by variation in our progress.

Everyone is on their own unique journey. Your path probably looks different from the people around you. Your responsibility is to trust God's leadership when the way becomes narrow, and you cannot see what is ahead. It doesn't matter if the person next to you has a similar experience. Keep reaching toward the goal God has given you. Don't forget that he knows exactly where you are, and he isn't worried about it.

Lord Jesus, keep me from comparing my life to others or getting stuck in the past. Help me reach forward toward the goal you've placed in front of me. Give me strength to persevere when I want to quit.

SEPTEMBER 18

Side by Side

*You stand beside me as my hero who rescues me.
I've seen with my own eyes the defeat of my enemies.
I've triumphed over them all!
Lord, it is so much better to trust in you to save me
than to put my confidence in someone else.*

PSALM 118:7-8 TPT

The strength and support of friends is powerful. They give us courage to continue, and they remind us we are not alone in this life. Even so, the encouragement of others is not our highest motivator. When no one else can help us, God is our rescuing hero. He stands by our side, and he doesn't leave us for even a second.

Though we may have a level of confidence in friends or family, the trust we have in the Lord can be greater still. He will never leave us or let us down. Even when our support system grows tired, goes home, or moves on to deal with their own challenges, God remains. He is steady and faithful, and he will always come through for us when needed.

Father, you are my ever-present help, and I trust you to do what no one else can. Stand beside me and rescue me when I need it. You alone are my hope.

Above All

Above all, keep fervent in your love for one another, because love covers a multitude of sins.

1 Peter 4:8 NASB

God's love is always pursuing us. It is faithful, active, kind, and sacrificial. His love is gracious, selfless, thoughtful, and steady. This is how we are meant to love others. There is so much power in God's love displayed between people. We have the ability to strengthen, lift up, and encourage each other. This is important on a daily basis, but it is arguably most important when people are struggling and overburdened.

The way you respond to the weaknesses of others is important. Love covers a multitude of sins. God is extraordinarily gracious with you, and he intends for you to do the same for others. When your ability to love is tested, this is when God can miraculously strengthen you to love as he does.

Lord, may I keep first thing's first and choose love whenever I have an option. Fill me with your love and strengthen me to love others well.

SEPTEMBER 20

Every Single Day

Surely goodness and mercy shall follow me
All the days of my life;
And I will dwell in the house of the Lord.

Psalm 23:6 NKJV

We can be confident in the Lord because he has proven that he is reliable. We can trust his character because it never wavers even when tested. We can have accurate expectations of him because he has shown that he keeps his promises. We know who he is, so we can be certain of what he has in store for us.

Scripture promises that goodness and mercy will follow you all of your days. This is a promise you can depend on you. Sometimes you will experience God's goodness externally, and sometimes you will experience it internally. He blesses his children in practical and spiritual ways. His gifts to us are not limited by our understanding.

God, surely your goodness and mercy will follow me all the days of my life. Help me stand firmly on that promise even when it doesn't look how I want. Give me an attitude of thanksgiving and eyes to see every good gift you give me.

SEPTEMBER 21

Unfolding Beauty

God has made everything beautiful for its own time. He has planted eternity in the human heart, but even so, people cannot see the whole scope of God's work from beginning to end.

ECCLESIASTES 3:11 NLT

God is not finished working in your life. Under the light of his love, you will continue to grow in his glorious presence. Don't despair over the parts of your life that seem unfinished or unresolved. God's timeline doesn't look like yours. You can trust him to make everything beautiful in its own time.

Your life is a precious journey. It is yours alone, and the Lord delights in leading you through it. Don't give up or lose heart. While you might feel weary sometimes, God does not tire of walking by your side. Though you cannot see the full scope of his work, you can be confident that he is in control.

Glorious One, thank you for the reminder that you are not finished with me yet. When I am discouraged, lift my eyes to see how far I've come. I trust you to shape my life into exactly what you want.

SEPTEMBER 22

Harbored Hope

They rejoiced when the waves grew quiet.
Then he guided them to the harbor they longed for.

Psalm 107:30 csb

God is our peace in the midst of chaos. He leads us through the tumultuous terrain of this world and brings stillness to the wind and waves. He cannot be intimidated or set off-track. He is capable of calming every storm. May we know his constant peace as he leads us to the harbor we long for.

God knows the desires of our hearts. Not only does he know them, but he cares about them. Life has many struggles, but with him there are also many breakthroughs. He provides breakthroughs of healing, of joy, peace, and victory. With God, all things are possible, and hope is never out of reach. Let's continue to trust him and rejoice when he settles our fears with the steadiness of his leadership.

Lord, I trust in your great name. You are my hope, peace, and comfort. Settle the storms in my life and lead me toward the safety I long for.

SEPTEMBER 23

Powerful Gift

> "When he, the Spirit of truth, comes, he will guide you into all the truth. He will not speak on his own; he will speak only what he hears, and he will tell you what is yet to come."
>
> JOHN 16:13 NIV

The Holy Spirit is a gift to us. In fact, Jesus said, that the Spirit is even better for us than his own presence. Jesus was limited by his humanity, but the Spirit of truth is not. The Spirit can be present in more than one place at a time. No matter where we are, the Spirit can lead us to God.

The Holy Spirit guides us into all truth. He reveals the heart of the Father and leads us in the ways of his kingdom. We can be confident that he is always with us, and we can trust him to teach us the ways of love. We need his guidance, comfort, encouragement, and help.

Holy Spirit, I'm so grateful for your persistent presence and incredible wisdom. Teach me more about God's character and guide me by the principles of his kingdom.

SEPTEMBER 24

Unwavering God

*The Lord is the everlasting God,
the Creator of the ends of the earth.
He does not faint or grow weary;
his understanding is unsearchable.*

Isaiah 40:28 ESV

God is everlasting; there was no beginning before him, and there is no end beyond him. All of time, space, and creation is wrapped up in his presence. It is almost impossible to understand how majestic, strong, and faithful he is. His understanding is beyond our capacity to comprehend. Still, he delights in revealing himself to those who seek him.

God never grows faint or weary. He does not get tired. This goes against our very nature because our limits are obvious. We need the nourishment of food and water to replenish our energy. We need rest, community, and shelter to thrive. God's personal resources are never lacking. Let's trust in his limitless power and unchanging character as he moves on our behalf.

Perfect God, I cannot fully understand you, but I've seen enough to believe that you are God, and you are good. You are worthy of my life, and I willingly lay it down before you.

SEPTEMBER 25

Promised Peace

I will listen to what God the Lord says;
he promises peace to his people, his faithful servants.

PSALM 85:8 NIV

When we turn the ears of our hearts to listen to the Lord, we will be met with the steadiness of his character. We will not find an impatient or indifferent God. When he speaks, his words are full of loving-kindness and truth. He promises peace to his faithful servants.

If you are his, you can be sure that this is a promise for you. When you follow his ways, he doesn't leave you wanting. When you devote your life to him, he will not disappoint you. Turning toward him is a daily practice. Each day is an opportunity to faithfully serve the Lord. He will uphold his promise, but don't forget the covenant you have made as well.

Prince of Peace, your ways are so much higher than mine. Give me grace to serve you faithfully. I don't want to insist on my own version of truth. Keep me close to your heart and protect me from wandering.

SEPTEMBER 26

Embrace the Promise

> These heroes all died still clinging to their faith, not even receiving all that had been promised them. But they saw beyond the horizon the fulfillment of their promises and gladly embraced it from afar. They all lived their lives on earth as those who belonged to another realm.
>
> HEBREWS 11:13 TPT

Not all promises are fulfilled in our lifetime. This is a hard reality to contend with, but it doesn't mean that God is not faithful. From everlasting to everlasting, he remains loyal to every vow he has made. Just because we don't see physical evidence of his work, doesn't mean it isn't happening.

We were not created for the short lives we will live. Our experience on earth is not the height of our reality. We belong in the realm of everlasting life. We belong in the kingdom of God where Christ rules and reigns. Let's embrace God's promise and live for that day. Our time on earth is fleeting, but God's promises are eternally good.

Lord, you are faithful and true. I believe that you will do all you have promised. I set my gaze on you, and I trust you to lead me toward eternal life.

SEPTEMBER 27

The Origin of All

In the beginning was the Word, and the Word was with God, and the Word was God. He was in the beginning with God. All things came into being through Him, and apart from Him not even one thing came into being that has come into being.

JOHN 1:1-3 NASB

God is the source of all living things. Through him, we live, move, and have our very being. He created us out of love, and he sustains us the same way. We were made by him, and we still find everything we need in his presence.

We don't have to turn to the right or the left to look for God. He is here with us. He is within us, and he surrounds us. He is our glorious Creator who joyfully inhabits his creation. He did not make us and leave us alone. We belong to him and with him. His presence is our home.

Father, open my eyes to the wonders of everything you've done. I cannot live without your presence. You are all I need. Give me grace to pursue you for all of my days.

SEPTEMBER 28

Still Working

> "My Father has been working until now,
> and I have been working."
>
> JOHN 5:17 NKJV

God is always at work. There's not a day when his loyal love is absent. There's not a moment when his grace cannot meet your needs. God doesn't tire, and he doesn't grow weary. He loves leading his children through life. He is happy to intervene on our behalf. He delights in what he does, and he does it well.

Just because you haven't seen the bigger picture of God's work doesn't mean that it's not underway. Ask him for a glimpse of what he is doing in your life and in the world at large. God is persistent, and he is not lazy. He will never give up orchestrating his perfect plans. His heart is for all to experience the life-giving redemption of his love, and he is constantly working toward that goal.

Lord, I'm so grateful you don't get tired of redeeming what is lost and fixing what is broken. Open my eyes to see your goodness and to recognize the ways you have been working in my own life.

SEPTEMBER 29

Completely Equipped

All Scripture is inspired by God and is profitable for teaching, for rebuking, for correcting, for training in righteousness, so that the man of God may be complete, equipped for every good work.

2 Timothy 3:16-17 csb

Every part of Scripture is valuable. It is an irreplaceable tool as we pursue living a life that honors God. His Word equips us for every good work, and it teaches us what his wisdom looks like. The Word offers conviction, correction, training, and encouragement.

We cannot overstate the importance of God's Word. It's a priceless gift that we should not take for granted. We can hold the very heart and intentions of God in our hands. We can flip through the pages and be reminded of his mercy and grace. For every problem we face, Scripture holds a solution. By storing the Word in our hearts, we set ourselves up for success in our journey of faith.

God, fill me with a greater desire to read the Word. Give me understanding as I study it and teach me how to apply it to my life. Bring truth to mind when I need encouragement or correction.

SEPTEMBER 30

Gracious Giving

Since you excel in so many ways—in your faith, your gifted speakers, your knowledge, your enthusiasm, and your love from us—I want you to excel also in this gracious act of giving.

2 CORINTHIANS 8:7 NLT

God loves when we use our gifts with confidence. We each have something beautiful to offer the body of Christ. Some of us are speakers, encouragers, teachers, and prophets. It's wonderful to excel in these good gifts. However, there are character traits of God that we should all exemplify. Generosity isn't limited to our specific gifts or talents. Everyone can grow in the gracious act of giving.

God is generous. His example is the one we follow. When we live with open hearts and hands, we reflect the generosity of God. There is so much love in the gracious act of giving. It is an opportunity to experience the powerful kindness of God in new ways and to keep our hearts soft in compassion.

Gracious God, I want to be more like you. Grow my heart in generosity. Show me opportunities to share what I have. I want to excel in gracious giving.

October

"My Presence will go with you,
and I will give you rest."

Exodus 33:14 NIV

OCTOBER 1

Encouraging Predictions

The one who prophesies speaks to people for their strengthening, encouraging and comfort.

1 CORINTHIANS 14:3 NIV

The gift of prophesy within the church is no small thing. It is meant to encourage, comfort, and strengthen us. When we understand its purpose, we can be mindful of wrongful displays of prophecy. Judgment, shame, and division are not works of God. Biblical prophecy does not produce those things.

The more we know God's nature, the more we are convinced of his love for us. If that is not clear through our speech to one another, then we have room to grow in his likeness. Let's be people who reflect the power of God through our words to one another. Whether we prophesy or simply speak words of life to each other, we can share God's heart by stirring up strength, encouragement, and comfort.

Lord, may I be someone who is known for clarity and kindness. I want to be an encourager who offers comfort, strength, and peace to those around me. Thank you for teaching me to be more like you.

OCTOBER 2

Secure Steps

*Whoever walks in integrity walks securely,
but he who makes his ways crooked will be found out.*

PROVERBS 10:9 ESV

The person of integrity has nothing to fear. They are honest and reliable. Their ways are consistent, and they follow through on their promises. Even when they make mistakes, they don't hide them. They admit when they are wrong, and they seek forgiveness and restoration.

The ways of the crooked are clear in people who lie to get ahead. They use manipulation to keep from being exposed, yet the truth cannot be hidden. Our true intentions will always be revealed. When we humbly walk in integrity, we don't need to hide our motives or our actions. We live in the light and are open to being seen.

Lord, give me strength to cultivate integrity in my life. Help me choose honesty when I am tempted to lie. Thank you for the security that comes from doing what is right.

OCTOBER 3

Living Message

You have been born again, and this new life did not come from something that dies, but from something that cannot die. You were born again through God's living message that continues forever.

1 PETER 1:23 NCV

The message of Christ is alive and well. The redemption power of God is at work today. Time has not weakened it or made it less effective. God's promises from thousands of years ago are relevant, powerful, and perfect. We can rely on him with confidence because he never changes.

The words of God bring life to us in the same way that rain and snow water the ground. God's living message is always potent. Everything he does is for our good and growth. May we receive the truth of the gospel and humble ourselves in light of God's love. His message to us lives forever. Let's walk under the power of God's loving leadership, for his ways will never fail.

Lord, speak to me today and bring greater freedom to my heart. You are the way, the truth, and the life. I will follow you for all my days.

OCTOBER 4

Holy Determination

*The LORD YAHWEH empowers me, so I am not humiliated.
For that reason, with holy determination,
I will do his will and not be ashamed.*

ISAIAH 50:7 TPT

As we follow the Lord in his loving ways, there is no reason to be ashamed. The truth of God's liberating mercy illuminates our minds and frees our hearts. There is grace, love, and understanding in the presence of God. He is the one who empowers us and keeps us steady.

We cannot be humiliated if we have nothing to hide. In contrast, where truth is lacking, the foundation is weak. Every lie is exposed at one time or another. Let's set our hearts with holy determination and trust God to defend us when the lying darts of the enemy are directed at us.

Faithful Father, you are a God of truth and justice. You will not let me be humiliated, and I will not hide in shame when your love has liberated me. Empower me today and give me strength to follow you no matter what.

OCTOBER 5

Such a Time as This

"If you keep silent at this time, liberation and rescue will arise for the Jews from another place, and you and your father's house will perish. And who knows whether you have not attained royalty for such a time as this?"

ESTHER 4:14 NASB

There are certain times in life we find ourselves at a crossroad. Not every correct choice is seamless or easy to make. In fact, it is especially difficult when the right thing is costly. For Esther, doing the right thing could mean losing her life. On the other hand, her silence could mean the death of many.

When faced with difficult choices, God gives us wisdom. He gives us strength to make decisions that honor him. The struggles we face are often opportunities to courageously follow God's plan. If we call upon him, he will open the right doors and equip us to walk through them. He will not leave us crushed under the weight of indecision.

God, I am trusting you for a breakthrough. You know the gravity of the decisions I have to make. Empower me by your grace and give me the wisdom necessary to honor you no matter what the cost is.

OCTOBER 6

In Christ

Be kind to one another, tenderhearted, forgiving one another, even as God in Christ forgave you.

EPHESIANS 4:32 NKJV

Why should we forgive one another when our pain runs deep? Why should we choose kindness over cold apathy? Why should we remain tenderhearted in a cruel world? The answer to each of these questions is found in Jesus. We give because we first received. We love because God loved us first.

Jesus is our example of how to live. If we want to be more like Christ, we must first acknowledge what we've received from him. He is tender toward us even on our worst day. He forgives us readily and fully when we humble ourselves in repentance. Why would we act any other way toward others? Because of God's great love for us, we can be loving.

Christ Jesus, help me love others as you have loved me. You have given me overwhelming mercy and grace in your presence. Help me extend the same sacrificial kindness toward others.

OCTOBER 7

Life-giving Light

In him was life, and that life was the light of men.

JOHN 1:4 CSB

Who of us, at one time or another, doesn't wonder at the deeper meaning of life? Maybe we feel stuck in the mundane aspects of our lives. Perhaps we have lost sight of what truly matters. No matter which direction our weary thoughts go, there is new life in Christ. He is the answer to every moment of despair. His life is a light to all.

Have you ever woken up in the middle of the night and felt like all hope was lost? Somehow, the break of day brings perspective you lacked in the dark. The light reminds you there is still hope, life, and beauty to experience. When you feel alone, lean into the fellowship of Christ. In him is the fullness of life. He will refresh your heart and renew your perspective.

Jesus, you are the light in my life. You break through the fog and rescue me from darkness. I look to you for perspective and truth. Thank you for pulling me from the depths and setting my feet on a firm foundation.

Immeasurable Love

> His unfailing love toward those who fear him
> is as great as the height of the heavens above the earth.
> He has removed our sins as far from us
> as the east is from the west.
>
> Psalm 103:11-12 NLT

When the love of God feels intangible or irrelevant, it's time for a fresh take. The truth of God doesn't change over time, but it can be illuminated in different ways. When the Holy Spirit brings understanding to our hearts, revelation often feels so simple yet incredibly profound.

Perhaps what you need today is to get outside and ask God to reveal the lengths of his love in different terms. Let the blue sky remind you that God's love reaches higher than the heavens. Let a lake or ocean remind you that nothing compares to the depths of his kindness. Creation is filled with reminders of the vastness of God's unfailing love.

Lord, I need a fresh revelation of your love. Remind me how great it is. You have changed my life, and I don't want to lose sight of that miracle.

OCTOBER 9

Glorious Grace

*May God be gracious to us and bless us
and make his face shine on us—
so that your ways may be known on earth,
your salvation among all nations.*

Psalm 67:1-2 NIV

Psalm 67 is a beautiful prayer to start or end the day. Our lives are reliant on the grace of God. The light of his face shines down on his people revealing the power of his ways and the incredible redemption of his love. He gives us everything we need to make it through this life and into his glorious kingdom.

Salvation is for all people everywhere. It is not reserved for some and excluded from others. God's glorious grace is incredibly generous, and there is always more. He shines his light equally on all creation. May your day begin and end with confidence that God is kind, and he longs for you to know him.

Gracious One, I want to grow in grace. May my life reflect your glory as I live humbly and openly before you. Thank you for the light of your love.

OCTOBER 10

Lifted Up

"As Moses lifted up the serpent in the wilderness, so must the Son of Man be lifted up, that whoever believes in him may have eternal life."

JOHN 3:14-15 ESV

The Lamb of God is our healing. He offers wholeness now and for eternity. Through him, our souls are secure. He is the one who brings breakthroughs and freedom. We no longer live under the shadow of sin, fear, or shame. Instead, we find our salvation, hope, and healing in him.

Look toward the Lamb no matter what you need relief from. He is not on a cross anymore. He is not in the grave either. He left the grip of death behind when he rose from the grave on the third day. He is alive, and his resurrection power is available to you.

Lamb of God, thank you for the power of your sacrifice. I look to you for all I need. Shine your light on me and lift my burdens.

OCTOBER 11

Grace and Peace

Grace and peace to you from God our Father and the Lord Jesus Christ.

1 Corinthians 1:3 NCV

God is gracious, kind, and present. He is powerful yet full of peace at all times. He is calm in every circumstance and steady through every trial. He is never worried, and he is never confused. He sees everything with full clarity and deep wisdom. We can trust him because he is our good Father.

May you know the grace and peace of God as you come and go. May you know the weight of his love on your life when you are awake or asleep. May you experience the peace of his presence when you work and when you rest. May you find confidence in him as you trust him and surrender to his ways.

God, thank you for the rest I find in your presence. Thank you for the grace and peace you've showered upon me. You are worthy of all my worship and praise.

OCTOBER 12

Living Sacrifice

> Beloved friends, what should be our proper response to God's marvelous mercies? To surrender yourselves to God to be his sacred, living sacrifices.
>
> ROMANS 12:1 TPT

The marvelous mercies of God transform our lives. God's love is great, and it changes us from the inside out. He has done marvelous things for those who follow him. The proper response to God's incredible mercy is to surrender ourselves before him and to live according to his law of love.

When we walk humbly before the Lord, we take on his ways as our own. We offer love because that is what he does. We forgive others because he forgave us. We give grace because we have received grace upon grace. We delight in justice because he is just and does what is right. It's an honor and a delight to live according to God's standards.

Faithful God, you are trustworthy and true. I offer you my life as a living sacrifice, not because I have to but because I get to. You are worthy of my devotion, and you win me over continually with your love.

OCTOBER 13

Arise and Build

I told them how the hand of my God had been favorable to me and also about the king's words which he had spoken to me. Then they said, "Let's arise and build." So they put their hands to the good work.

NEHEMIAH 2:18 NASB

We were not made to lead meaningless lives. We were not made to be stagnant or purposeless. God has given each of us specific work to do. When we put our hands to God's work it is not tiresome, lonely, or burdensome. We were created to support each other and operate as a body rather than individually. We thrive when we work together for the glory of God.

There are people across the entire world who are dedicating their work to God. We don't have to look far to find believers who have devoted their lives to advancing God's kingdom. Instead of repeating what's already occurring, we can partner together. We can combine our efforts and work without jealousy or the search for status. Look at how God has gifted you and put your hands to the work of the kingdom.

God, I want to partner with your purposes and see the body of Christ work together. Give me vision for your plans and show me opportunities to join in what you are doing around the world.

OCTOBER 14

Abide

"Abide in Me, and I in you. As the branch cannot bear fruit of itself, unless it abides in the vine, neither can you, unless you abide in Me."

JOHN 15:4 NKJV

Though we may feel pressure to perform, God invites us into a peaceful partnership with him. Our striving can cease, and we can be our truest selves. When we abide in Christ, we are dependent on his presence. His love fuels our lives. It offers nourishment to our hearts, minds, and bodies. Our greatest strength is found resting in our connection to God.

We can't produce good fruit on our own. That means any good fruit in this weary world comes from the work of God in his people. Let's find our rest in the powerful presence of God which brings redemption, mercy, and renewal. His life flowing into us brings goodness for all. As we abide in him, we find beauty, peace, care, and joy.

Lord, you are my resting place. I don't have to try harder to produce good fruit if I simply allow your love to move through my life. Thank you for the life you continually offer.

OCTOBER 15

No Condemnation

When Jesus stood up, he said to her, "Woman, where are they? Has no one condemned you?"
"No one, Lord," she answered.
"Neither do I condemn you," said Jesus. "Go, and from now on do not sin anymore."

JOHN 8:10-11 CSB

Jesus constantly displayed tenderhearted mercy. He paid close attention to people the world declared worthless. His kindness challenged the wise and liberating the oppressed. The way Jesus treated vulnerable people is worth our attention. If we are called to follow his example, we can't skip over his gentle and deliberate care for the needy.

There are plenty of people who are quick to condemn others while overlooking their own flaws. These are the people who were challenged by Jesus' actions. In the end, they walked away when confronted with their own inadequacy. Let's align ourselves with God and offer compassion and relief rather than condemnation, for that is what we receive from him.

Gracious God, may I be quick to choose compassion over judgment. Remind me of all you've done for me and help me be merciful toward others.

OCTOBER 16

Turn and Live

> "I don't want you to die," says the Sovereign LORD.
> "Turn back and live!"
>
> EZEKIEL 18:32 NLT

God's heart for us is that we will live. While the enemy has plans to steal, kill, and destroy, God has plans for us to have a rich and satisfying life. This doesn't mean our lives will be overflowing with material gain, but he wants us to know the abundance of his goodness. His ways lead to life, and his wisdom never fails. Everything he does is intended for our good.

God doesn't want your life to be defined by death, depression, or despair. While you will surely experience suffering or grief, he doesn't want your heart to be in a constant state of overwhelm. He offers you hope, peace, and joy even when your circumstances are difficult. Your relationship with him is not meant to be one of your struggles. Surrender your heart to him and expect him to meet you in life-giving ways.

Sovereign Lord, I don't want my life to be filled with shame, despair, and death. Fill me with life once again. Draw me back to you and water the dry parts of my life. Soften my heart as I cling to you. You are my hope.

OCTOBER 17

Lifelong Friend

*Because he turned his ear to me,
I will call on him as long as I live.*

PSALM 116:2 NIV

The beauty of God's friendship is that it is not fickle. His relationship with us is long-lasting. We can join with the psalmist and call on him as long as we live. There's no reason to withhold our prayers from him, for he is near to all who call on him.

God's response to us doesn't depend on how long we've known him. He always answers the cries of his children. He doesn't hold grudges against us or punish us for our mistakes. He lovingly teaches, corrects, and guides us as we follow his lead. It is never too early or late to turn our hearts toward him. He is our Savior and friend, and his faithfulness is displayed by everything he does. He deserves our wholehearted trust.

Lord, I won't stay away from you today. I draw near, speaking to you as I do my closest friends. I want to know more about you and experience the power of your presence.

OCTOBER 18

Enduring Righteousness

"He has distributed freely, he has given to the poor; his righteousness endures forever."

2 CORINTHIANS 9:9 ESV

God gives freely. His actions always line up with his overwhelmingly generous nature. His righteousness stands from generation to generation. He loves his children without discrimination. He lavishes his love on the rich and poor alike. Though many may misunderstand or underestimate him, the truth of his power remains.

Jesus Christ is our righteousness, and he will endure forever. We are not perfect, but we can walk in the confidence of his loving redemption that sets us free and gives us peace. There is no greater example to follow in all the world than the loving lead of Jesus our Savior. He is worthy of all our love and devotion.

Righteous One, no one can diminish your goodness. Thank you for the power of your saving grace. You redeemed me, and your righteousness will endure forever.

OCTOBER 19

Happy Trust

> The LORD gives us kindness and honor.
> He does not hold back anything good
> from those whose lives are innocent.
>
> PSALM 84:11 NCV

We are made innocent by humbly surrendering to the love of God. He transforms our hearts and lives completely. We are renewed by his kindness, and we are given an unmerited seat at his table. He honors us even though he is the only one truly deserving of honor. He does not hold back anything good from us.

There may be struggles we cannot outrun, but God's goodness outlasts them all. We are happy when we follow him because he is faithful and true. He fulfills his promises, and he lovingly shows up when we need him. He is compassionate toward our weakness, and he is eager for us to know how much he loves us. There is no better way to live than openly, honestly, and humbly before him.

Lord, there is nothing you cannot do. I have tasted and seen that you are good. Meet me today and equip me to honor you in all I do. You are worthy of everything I have.

OCTOBER 20

Joyful Kingdom

"As you passionately seek his kingdom, above all else, he will supply your needs. So don't ever be afraid, dearest friends! Your loving Father joyously gives you his kingdom with all its promises!"

Luke 12:31-32 TPT

The passionate pursuit of God is rewarded with the confident peace of his presence. There is joy in his heart, and he doesn't hesitate to share it. He doesn't provide for his people out of obligation, but he delights in taking care of those who trust him. He loves sharing the abundance of his kingdom with his children.

How have you experienced God's provision? What do you need God's help with today? Lay your worries at his feet and tell him what you need. Don't be ashamed, and don't hold back. May you be met by the incomparable sweetness of his nature. He loves you and he longs to take care of you. He is an attentive Father who joyously gives you what you need most.

Father, I'm so glad I can come to you as a child and not like a beggar. Bless me with the peace of your presence. I trust you to meet my needs because you know what is best. I put my life in your hands.

OCTOBER 21

He Is Greater

You are from God, little children, and have overcome them; because greater is He who is in you than he who is in the world.

1 JOHN 4:4 NASB

If we want to follow Jesus, we must embrace the values of God's kingdom. Our actions should be rooted in love and defined by gracious mercy. We don't overcome problems the same way the world does. We refuse to lie, undercut others, or operate with selfish ambition. Instead, we honor God by imitating Jesus.

Little children often copy what their parents do. As children of God, we can do the same. As we model our lives after the life of Jesus, we will become more and more like him. We partner with God when we love others and sacrificially serve them. We submit ourselves to God's ways rather than the worlds ways, and we are confident that we won't be disappointed.

God, you have overcome the world, and I put my faith in you. Your love stands strong in the face of evil and deception. Give me grace to imitate you in everything I do.

OCTOBER 22

Alive Forevermore

> "I am He who lives, and was dead, and behold, I am alive forevermore. Amen. And I have the keys of Hades and of Death."
>
> REVELATION 1:18 NKJV

The book of Revelation outlines John's depiction of the end times. Jesus spoke to John through an incredible vision, sharing the mysteries of what is still to come when he returns. Jesus is as needed, relevant, and wise as he always was. We are still desperately waiting for him to make all things right. Our highest hope is still in his final redemption.

Jesus holds the keys of death in his hands. He will liberate every soul that is written in the book of life, leading them into the joy of his eternal kingdom. Just as Jesus is alive forevermore, his people will dwell in the beauty of his kingdom forever. May we find rest, peace, courage, and assurance in this promised hope.

Lord Jesus, I need the deep assurance of your living love to transform my heart and perspective. Thank you for the promise of what is to come. Meet me today and renew my strength.

OCTOBER 23

Immovable Kingdom

Since we are receiving a kingdom that cannot be shaken, let us be thankful. By it, we may serve God acceptably, with reverence and awe, for our God is a consuming fire.

HEBREWS 12:28-29 CSB

When we are kingdom-minded, we will remember the hope that lies beyond sight. The kingdom of God cannot be shaken. Though the world is in constant flux, the kingdom of God remains steady. God's nature doesn't change, and neither does the salvation of our souls.

God is a consuming fire. Everything is purified and clarified in his presence. Temporary things burn up, but the things that were built to last only become stronger. Our sin, shame, and fear are burned in his presence. At the same time, hope, peace, joy, and love are magnified. Let's stand upon the unshakable attributes of God and his kingdom while we serve him with our whole hearts.

Lord, in a world where nothing seems to last, my heart is rooted in the steadfastness of your love. I'm so grateful that your kingdom cannot be shaken.

OCTOBER 24

There's a Way

The temptations in your life are no different from what others experience. And God is faithful. He will not allow the temptation to be more than you can stand. When you are tempted, he will show you a way out so that you can endure.

1 Corinthians 10:13 NLT

None of us are exempt from experiencing temptation. We might have different weaknesses, but we will all have to face them at some point. God has not left us to fend for ourselves. When we are tempted, he invites us to lean on him. He longs to give us endurance and strength. He offers us a way out, but we have to take him up on it.

If we are tempted and refuse God's help, we are the creators of our own problems. We cannot claim that we are too weak or that the temptation was too strong. If we want to experience freedom, we must acknowledge God's faithfulness and run to him without shame. He is not afraid of reaching into the dark places of our lives. He longs for us to accept his offer of help.

Lord, I trust you to lead me in truth and love. When I face temptation, help me turn to you quickly. You already know my weakness, and I don't need to be ashamed. Give me courage to endure.

OCTOBER 25

Declarations of Faith

If you declare with your mouth, "Jesus is Lord," and believe in your heart that God raised him from the dead, you will be saved.

Romans 10:9 NIV

Simple faith paired with a wholehearted declaration is enough to know Jesus and experience his salvation. If we believe that Jesus is the Son of God, and we declare that he rose from the dead, our lives are surrendered to his lordship. There is no need to overcomplicate the good news. We have been saved by a simple and glorious gospel.

God intended for his plan to be easily grasped. He didn't make it difficult or impossible to find the truth. We don't have to be scholars to understand the glory of what he's done. The way to salvation is accessible to everyone. When we feel weary or confused, we can find relief in focusing on the basic truth of Jesus and the redemption he provides.

Savior, I want to know more about you. Your saving grace has set me free, and I find my rest in you. When I am overwhelmed, confused, or frustrated, remind me of the simple truth I can depend on.

OCTOBER 26

Increasing Wisdom

Jesus increased in wisdom and in stature and in favor with God and man.

Luke 2:52 ESV

When the Son of God first came to the earth, he was born a baby. He didn't come as a full-grown man, or as a glorified king ready to rule and reign. He humbled himself to experience humanity in the same way we do. As Jesus grew, he increased in wisdom, stature, and in favor with God and man. His capacity changed as he went from infant, to boy, to adolescent, to adult.

If Jesus had to increase in wisdom and stature, how much more should we expect the same? We don't need to stay stagnant in our understanding, and we don't need to be ashamed of progress over perfection. We gain maturity as we humbly admit when we are wrong and choose to change our ways. Let's not grow weary of seasons of transition that stretch us beyond our capacity. Growth is always a good thing.

Lord, thank you for the reminder that growing, learning, and changing is a lifelong pursuit. I follow your lead, Jesus. Help me be flexible and eager to learn in every stage of life.

OCTOBER 27

Chosen First

"You did not choose me, but I chose you and appointed you that you should go and bear fruit and that your fruit should abide, so that whatever you ask the Father in my name, he may give it to you."

JOHN 15:16 ESV

If there is any pull in our hearts to serve the Lord, we can be assured that God put it there. Before we even know him, Jesus chose us. His sacrificial love draws us in and transforms our hearts. He is gentle in his approach, and his kindness is magnetic. We partner with him because we are confident in his character. We run to him because he calls us first.

We get to choose how we respond to God. We get to choose whether we will live in submission to his love or not. We don't have to surrender to him because he has given us free will. At the end of the day, we get to decide if he is worthy of our lives. Our response to God isn't guaranteed, but his response to us is. He will not change his mind. His love is loyal, and his covenant cannot be broken.

Father, it baffles me how your love is so steady and sure. You don't waver in kindness, mercy, or justice. Give me grace to have the same level of steadiness. I respond to you with confidence because you are worthy.

OCTOBER 28

He Already Knows

"Your Father knows the things you need before you ask him."
MATTHEW 6:8 NCV

Before we even know to ask, God sees our needs. He knows what we need in every circumstance. Not only is he aware of us, but he cares deeply for us. He isn't a God who sees and walks away. He is ready to provide for us when we call upon him. Where we are lacking, he is eager to step in.

As a good Father, God takes care of his children. We can trust him to provide for us. As he does, we can selflessly take care of others. We can treat the people around us with generosity because God has been so generous with us. We can share our resources because God has not withheld provision from us. If God readily and joyfully meets our needs, we should do the same for others when possible.

Father, thank you for providing for my needs. There is peace in trusting you, and there is rest in the assurance of your faithfulness. Help me care for the people around me as you have cared for me.

OCTOBER 29

Sound of Brilliance

*The God of gods, the mighty Lord himself, has spoken!
He shouts out over all the people of the earth
in every brilliant sunrise and every beautiful sunset,
saying, "Listen to me!"*

PSALM 50:1 TPT

Every brilliant sunrise is a word of the Lord. Every beautiful sunset is a glorious shout of his faithfulness. There is so much to learn about God from clues hidden in creation. Stars light up the sky at night, and they speak of his splendor. Tides rise and fall with the moon, and they remind us of the cycles of life.

There is a tender fellowship with God in nature. Let's not ignore the invitation to stand in awe of who he is. Let's slow down and give our attention to the smallest details of creation. Each intricate system and ecosystem tell us about God's character. He is creative, precise, and more intelligent than we can comprehend. God is speaking through creation if we will just take the time to listen.

Creator, fill me with awe and appreciation for all you have made. When I am astounded by the complexity of nature, speak to me about your character. I am listening!

OCTOBER 30

Divine Perceptions

Since the creation of the world His invisible attributes, that is, His eternal power and divine nature, have been clearly perceived, being understood by what has been made, so that they are without excuse.

ROMANS 1:20 NASB

God's glory is on display for all to see. He is not hiding from us. He has given us a world full of evidence that points toward his perfection, creativity, and beauty. We can look forward to the fullness of God to come, and we can eagerly notice the fingerprints of his character that are already here.

God's beauty can be seen in the way the sun shines through the leaves on a crisp Autumn day. It can be seen in the soft chirping of birds, and in the grace of water as it flows. There are so many things we can learn about our Creator as we pay attention to creation. Let's not overlook the wonders of this world, for they are awe-inducing for a reason! They speak of the one who created them all, and his beauty is unrivaled.

Lord, creation speaks of your wonder and majesty! Show me more of who you are. Open my eyes to see your glory in the world around me.

OCTOBER 31

Everywhere You Look

*He loves righteousness and justice;
The earth is full of the goodness of the Lord.*

Psalm 33:5 nkjv

Studies now back up what we already know to be true; when we look for reasons to be grateful, we will find them. When we look with eyes of expectation, we will notice what we might have missed otherwise. The simple act of paying attention trains our brains to look more closely for evidence.

The more we practice gratitude, the easier it becomes. Eventually we will find ourselves automatically noticing the good over the bad. There is so much hardship in the world, but there is also so much beauty. There is goodness and evidence of God's mercy. There is joy and glimpses of the perfection for which we were made. We only have to pay attention in order to see it.

God, the earth is full of your goodness. I don't want to live bogged down by the weight of worries when there is an invitation to a better way. Give me eyes to see evidence of your beauty, joy, kindness, and mercy.

November

My flesh and my heart may fail,
but God is the strength of my heart
and my portion forever.

PSALM 73:26 NIV

NOVEMBER 1

Remarkable

> I will praise you
> because I have been remarkably and wondrously made.
> Your works are wondrous,
> and I know this very well.
>
> PSALM 139:14 CSB

When God created you, he could have done anything. You are exactly what he wanted at that moment. You are the expression of his delight, and he loves how he made you. Though you may struggle to see past the flaws you so readily focus on, God's love for you is complete.

The fact that you are here in this world is a miracle. The DNA shared by your parents could have combined in a multitude of ways, and your existence is uniquely beautiful. You were remarkably wonderfully made. God chose to create you exactly as you are, and his works are awe inspiring. It is not prideful to be thankful for how God made you. You are the apple of his eye, and you can fully embrace his opinion of you!

Maker, thank you for creating me as I am. Give me grace to love myself as fully as you do. In your love I come alive!

NOVEMBER 2

Honorable Gifts

"Look at the lilies and how they grow. They don't work or make their clothing, yet Solomon in all his glory was not dressed as beautifully as they are."

Luke 12:27 NLT

The lilies of the field are beautiful. Each wildflower is unique and wonderfully dressed just as God designed them. If he adorns the fields, he won't overlook you. God will not neglect your basic needs. He will provide for you out of the abundance of his kingdom.

If you do nothing else today, lean into the love of your Father. Get to know his heart for you. What is it that he wants to show you today? How does he want to pour his love on you? Invite him to show you the glory of his provision and the beauty of his kindness toward you. He wants you to know you are taken care of.

God, I am relieved that I don't have to work hard to know you. I don't have to strive to earn your love. Show me what you have for me today.

NOVEMBER 3

Words of Life

"The Spirit gives life; the flesh counts for nothing. The words I have spoken to you—they are full of the Spirit and life."

JOHN 6:63 NIV

The physical world isn't the only reality. There are spiritual things at play beyond the surface of our awareness. The values of God's kingdom matter in the physical world, but they go beyond it. The foundations of the earth were built upon God and his nature.

The Spirit offers life to the soul and brings inner awakening and strength of heart and mind. If we only look at the physical things around us, we remain shortsighted. God's perspective is higher, broader, and wiser than ours. The Spirit offers us life-giving vision and encouragement to perceive what God offers in the everlasting realm of his kingdom.

Lord, speak your life-giving words straight from your Spirit to my own. Increase my understanding of your kingdom ways and your powerful nature.

Close Comfort

"I, I am he who comforts you;
who are you that you are afraid of man who dies,
of the son of man who is made like grass."

Isaiah 51:12 ESV

God is not intimidated by the threats of men. He cannot be manipulated by shows of power or wealth. He remains steadfast, true, and close to all who look for him. His power is strong enough to save our souls and redeem us from the grip of death. His power heals the sick, tends to the brokenhearted, and even raises the dead to life again!

God's comfort is always available to us. He will not leave us in our time of need. Let's lean into the peace of his love. He will soothe our grief in his presence. When we are afraid, let's turn our attention to the God who never fails. Even when we cannot see the way out, God is with us in tangible grace. He is our close comfort!

Comforter, may I know the tangible peace of your presence which passes all understanding. Come close to me as I lean toward you today.

NOVEMBER 5

Declared Innocent

Those who are in Christ Jesus are not judged guilty.

ROMANS 8:1 NCV

If God is for us, who can be against us? If God has removed the guilt of sin and shame, why would we take on the yoke of it again? Let's never allow the voice of doubt to lead us away from the powerfully liberating love of God. Through Jesus, we are set free.

When we yield our lives to the Lord, he sets us free from the chains that once bound us. Eternal life is ours when we confess that Jesus is God's son, and he rose from the dead. There is nothing for us to fear when we live in the light of God's love. Let's throw off the distractions that keep us stuck and live in the freedom we've been given.

Lord, you are the ultimate judge of all. I humble myself before you and want nothing more than the freedom you offer. Show me the lengths of your mercy in greater measure today.

NOVEMBER 6

Heaping Portions

From the overflow of his fullness we received grace heaped upon more grace!

JOHN 1:16 TPT

There is more than enough for everyone at God's banquet table. There is overflowing goodness and everything we need for life and godliness. There are heaps of grace, mounds of joy, and endless amounts of lavish love. God's generous portions allow us to overflow and be generous with others.

In a world full of limitations, it can be difficult to imagine such bounty. We have to be careful not to apply our own limitations to God. There are no limits in his kingdom. In the Lord, there is always abundance. He never runs out of patience or wisdom. There is always more than enough.

King of heaven, thank you for giving me access to your table of plenty. I come with open arms and a humble heart to receive from the overflow of your fullness. Thank you.

NOVEMBER 7

Revived by God's Word

> This is my comfort in my misery,
> That Your word has revived me.
>
> PSALM 119:50 NASB

There is energy in God's Word. The right word spoken at the right time brings restoration and new life. The comfort, wisdom, peace, and encouragement found in the Word can shift the atmosphere of our day. There is life energy in God's Word regardless of our circumstances.

Even our most helpful tools will not meet every need, but God knows exactly how to provide for us. His Word is relevant and timely. Ask the Lord to speak to you right now, and he will meet you. Let his Word revive you as you tune your heart to his voice. He is ready to speak directly and clearly. Take time to listen and be refreshed.

God, you know exactly what I need right now. Give me a fresh portion of truth to satisfy my heart. I am listening for your voice.

Steady Presence

"The LORD, He is the One who goes before you. He will be with you, He will not leave you nor forsake you; do not fear nor be dismayed."

DEUTERONOMY 31:8 NKJV

For every reason we have to fear, there is an even greater reason to trust the one who never leaves us. He goes before us into every situation and makes a way. He will be with us through every twist and turn of the path we are on. As we rely on him, he offers everything we need exactly when we need it.

You don't have to carry the weight of the world or even your own responsibilities alone. God is willing to carry your burdens and give you respite when you need it. Rely on his leadership and take each step as it comes. He has paved a way for you, and he knows what is best. He is fully aware of your movement, and he will not let your foot slip.

Faithful One, thank you for your promised presence and help. You are my courage, comfort, and confidence. Strengthen my faith and keep my eyes on you.

NOVEMBER 9

Quiet Confidence

I love the LORD because he has heard my appeal for mercy.

PSALM 116:1 CSB

There is relief in knowing that God hears us and answers our cries for mercy. He is ready to help in times of trouble. He is a reliable Savior who never abandons us. When our hearts are convinced of his help, we don't waste time or energy worrying. With quiet and wholehearted trust, we wait confidently for God to make a way where there seems to be none.

Take every opportunity to lavish love on God. When your heart is stirred to worship him don't sweep it away. Look toward him and offer him your thanks. As you engage with him in praise, you will become even more convinced of his faithfulness. As you acknowledge his goodness, you will grow in dependence upon him.

Lord, thank you for hearing every prayer and plea. You are my ready help and my close companion. I love you!

NOVEMBER 10

Overwhelming Success

Overwhelming victory is ours through Christ, who loved us.
ROMANS 8:37 NLT

If we measure our success by the world's standards, we will always be grasping for perfection. Success is a moving target for most of us because the requirements are always changing. Those who achieve success in the eyes of the world may still feel like they're lacking.

God doesn't promise us a life without struggles or suffering. Our circumstances won't always be perfect, but God's standard of success is our measuring line. There is greater victory in Christ than can be achieved through the world. His love is our highest aim. His presence is our greatest priority. We will be fully satisfied when we devote our lives to Him.

Lord, may I define my success by knowing you and being known by you. I want to live in the power of your love every day. You are my greatest hope and my outstanding peace.

NOVEMBER 11

Unending Peace

> He comforts us in all our troubles so that we can comfort others. When they are troubled, we will be able to give them the same comfort God has given us.
>
> 2 Corinthians 1:4 NLT

God comforts us in all our troubles. He does not forget a single one. It doesn't matter if other people think our troubles are significant or not. God sees our pain, and he offers encouragement without judgment. He is gentle and kind even when the world is harsh and critical. He holds us closely and mercifully speaks truth over us. His comfort does not come with a hidden agenda or selfish ambition.

God comforts you so you can comfort others. He is gracious and merciful toward you so you can extend the same kindness to those around you. As he loves you, he increases your capacity to share his love with the people around you. You have the privilege of being a healing presence in the lives of others.

Comforter, show me how I can be supportive of the people around me. Teach me how to comfort others as you've comforted me. Give me wisdom to say the right words and patience to be gentle with those who are suffering.

Promise of Restoration

After you have suffered a little while, the God of all grace, who has called you to his eternal glory in Christ, will himself restore, confirm, strengthen, and establish you.

1 Peter 5:10 ESV

If we are not watchful, we may miss the compromise that pulls at our hearts. If we don't fill our minds with truth, we may begin to mistrust who God is. If we are not mindful of how the world's standards impact us, we may become convinced that God is limited or unreliable.

It's not easy to remain steady in the midst of evil and suffering. It's tempting to give in to popular habits, beliefs, and patterns. God knows how trying it can be to stay faithful in our current society. He knows that it is a challenge, and he knows that sometimes we suffer. He promises that our trials won't last forever. After a while, he will restore, confirm, strengthen, and establish us. In the meantime, we can rely on his persistent peace and faithful love.

Gracious God, I won't turn to the right or to the left today. I set my gaze upon you, and I trust you. Walk with me and abide in me. Strengthen me and help me remain faithful.

NOVEMBER 13

Better Help

"I tell you the truth, it is better for you that I go away. When I go away, I will send the Helper to you. If I do not go away, the Helper will not come."

JOHN 16:7 NCV

Jesus knew what was best for his disciples and for everyone who would follow him in the days to come. He knew that the Holy Spirit was the gift we all needed. In order for us to receive the fullness of the Spirit, Jesus had to return to the Father. He left so that we could have everything we really need.

The ministry of the Spirit is thorough and accurate. He brings revelation to the hearts of men and women. He reminds us of what is true, and he equips us to stay faithful to Jesus until his return. He ministers life and hope when we need it most. Without him we would be left to our own devices and wisdom. Through his fellowship we have access to the perfect and eternal wisdom of God.

Holy Spirit, your fellowship is a great gift, and I do not take it for granted. Speak because I am listening. Remind me of the truth when I forget and encourage me when I am weary.

NOVEMBER 14

Unshakable Hope

Our hope for you is unshakable, because we know that just as you share in our sufferings you will also share in God's comforting strength.

2 CORINTHIANS 1:7 TPT

Where there is suffering there is also the opportunity to receive God's comfort. He lovingly gives us strength when we cannot muster it up on our own. Instead of facing our suffering with despair, fear, or doubt, we can expect the Lord's present peace and love to meet us in it.

The presence of pain reminds us that things aren't the way they're supposed to be. When everything feels wrong, we find hope in the knowledge that perfection is coming. There is a breakthrough for each of us as we submit our lives to the Lord and trust him with our hearts and lives. Let's rejoice in our sufferings and weaknesses because we know that God can restore and redeem everything.

God, empower my heart and give me strength to endure. My hope is in you, and you are my greatest source of comfort. When I am suffering, remind me that I'm not alone.

NOVEMBER 15

By Name

*Raise your eyes on high
And see who has created these stars,
The One who brings out their multitude by number,
He calls them all by name.*

ISAIAH 40:26 NASB

God created the planets, moons, stars, and galaxies, and he calls them each by name. If the creator of all things can call each starry host by name, how much more can we be assured of his knowledge of us? He is intimately aware of every aspect of his creation. None of us are overlooked or ignored.

There are one hundred billion stars in our galaxy alone. If you were to guess how many there are in the entire universe, the number would be even more staggering. Be encouraged that the God who named each of the stars in the sky calls you by name. You are even more precious to him than the awe-inducing night sky. You are not lost in this great world. Find your home in his presence where his love and mercy are unlimited.

Creator, I cannot begin to imagine how many stars exist, and it astounds my heart to know that you call them each by name. Your love is beyond my understanding! Your mercy and grace are beyond my wildest dreams!

NOVEMBER 16

God's Timing

> The vision is yet for an appointed time;
> But at the end it will speak, and it will not lie.
> Though it tarries, wait for it;
> Because it will surely come,
> It will not tarry.
>
> HABAKKUK 2:3 NKJV

When we are young, time seems to drag on. We haven't yet learned the value of patience. As we grow older, we learn that there is wisdom in trusting God's timing. There is no rush in his kingdom. There is space to move, rest, and trust. This is something we all must learn, and it applies as much to spiritual things as to physical.

It can be discouraging when God's timing doesn't line up with our preferences. We don't have to make his promises happen. He will work them out in his timing, and we have only to trust him. As we do, we can put our energy toward what is in our ability to control. There's no point in worrying over whether or not God will show up on time. He is never late.

Lord, you are faithful and true, and you will accomplish all you set out to do. Help me rest in trust, abide in hope, and wait with patience.

NOVEMBER 17

Fully Enriched

The One who provides seed for the sower and bread for food will provide and multiply your seed and increase the harvest of your righteousness, as you are enriched in every way for all generosity, which produces thanksgiving to God through us.

2 CORINTHIANS 9:10-11 CSB

Seasons of abundance and fruitfulness are so exciting! Alongside being thankful, we must remember that God has given us instructions for abundance. We are meant to share our blessings generously. God does not bless us so we can keep it all to ourselves. He intends for us to take care of others.

Which area of your life has abundance right now? Do you have extra time, money, skills, or emotional capacity? There are a multitude of ways to share the gifts God has given you. Wherever you have extra, remember to hold it loosely and look for opportunities to give it away. Don't store it up for the future or relish it yourself. There is so much power in partnering with God through generosity.

Generous One, thank you for your powerful example of lavish generosity. I don't take it for granted, and I open my heart and hands in practical ways to share what I have been blessed with. Give me grace to share with a cheerful heart.

NOVEMBER 18

Even in Trouble

There is a time and a way for everything, even when a person is in trouble.

ECCLESIASTES 8:6 NLT

Even when a person is in trouble, it does not spell doom. This is important to keep in mind in this age full of overwhelming stories of constant trouble around the world. It is too much for any of us to handle, and we are not meant to. Our worry doesn't have an impact, but Jesus can change everything.

When we trust God, we don't have to turn a blind eye to the reality of trouble. Instead, we turn our eyes toward the only one who can make a difference. We trust God with the things that are far beyond our capacity to fix. If there is a way for us to help, he will show us. If there's none, we leave it in his hands. Either way, the answer to our troubles is to trust God.

Lord, may my heart find rest in the confidence of your care. Even in trouble, you provide solutions and peace. I look to you instead of worrying.

Higher Ways

*"As the heavens are higher than the earth,
so are my ways higher than your ways
and my thoughts than your thoughts."*

ISAIAH 55:9 NIV

How often do we need to be reminded of God's faithfulness? There is no shame in admitting it may be more often than we hope. His faithfulness does not depend on our consistency. He is fully aware that his ways are higher than ours. He knows that we will falter, and he assures us that he never will.

When we struggle to understand, let's look at the one who sees clearly. His perspective is above the chaotic fray of the world. When our lives feel like a tangled mess, he can easily see the way out. His intentions toward us are good and his ability is proven. We can trust him to show us the way to go. If we let him, he will faithfully lead us both physically and spiritually.

Constant One, I needed to remember your perfect perspective today. I'm thankful for your ability to do everything well. You know what is best and I trust you. Lead me along the path you have chosen for my life.

NOVEMBER 20

Heartfelt Song

*The LORD is my strength and my shield;
in him my heart trusts, and I am helped;
my heart exults,
and with my song I give thanks to him.*

PSALM 28:7 ESV

Music has the power to convey our emotions in a way that goes beyond our brains and bodies. Sometimes we can sing from the depths of our soul more effectively than we can communicate otherwise. Our melodies reach the ears of our Father and delight his heart. He loves listening to the songs of his children.

Every psalm we read was written as a song. There is so much to glean from their poetry, but there is also so much depth to feel when they are set to music. They become more than the sum of their words. If you've never done it before, pick a favorite psalm and sing it instead of reading it. You could make up a melody to it or check if someone else has done it already. Offer your song to the Lord with thanksgiving.

Lord, I will sing to you today, for you are worthy of my praise. I lift my voice to you and trust that you see my heart.

NOVEMBER 21

The Right Time

*"At the right time I heard your prayers.
On the day of salvation I helped you."
I tell you that the "right time" is now, and the "day of
salvation" is now.*

2 CORINTHIANS 6:2 NCV

Though there are certain things we must wait for, God's presence is not one of them. By the power of the Holy Spirit, we are never without his presence. He is always with us just as he promised he would be. When we call on him, he reminds us that he has never left our side.

God hears our prayers and brings salvation. Not a moment goes by where we are without his presence. Today is the day of salvation. Find your hope and strength in God right now. There is no reason to wait. He offers you the abundance of his kingdom without delay. Allow yourself to rest in his presence and take hold of everything he has promised you.

Lord Jesus, you are my salvation. You are my assurance of hope. I have cried out to you, and you have answered. All that I am looking for is already found in you.

NOVEMBER 22

Secure Faith

They will not live in fear or dread of what may come, for their hearts are firm, ever secure in their faith.

PSALM 112:7 TPT

When our hearts are rooted in the faithfulness of God, there is no reason to live in fear. This is a powerful and liberating truth, yet how many of us truly live this way? Let's abandon our worries as we give them over to God. He is faithful to do all that he promised. His love never leaves us even when our biggest fears present themselves.

When the worst happens, God is with us. There is always peace, love, and joy in the Holy Spirit. There is promised restoration and redemption for our greatest losses. No matter what comes, God is faithful. Though we may suffer, our hope cannot be taken away because it secured in God's everlasting and unshakeable kingdom.

Lord, I give you all the fear, anxiety, worry, and dread that has tried to take root in my heart. I leave it with you, and I trust you to take care of me.

NOVEMBER 23

Receive with Gratitude

Everything created by God is good, and nothing is to be rejected if it is received with gratitude; for it is sanctified by means of the word of God and prayer.

1 Timothy 4:4-5 NASB

This scripture speaks about which foods are considered clean or unclean. Paul is trying to communicate that our attitude matters more than our actions. He is saying that if we eat something with gratitude, it becomes clean. The heart of the matter is that the food we eat isn't worth fighting about.

We can take this principle to heart by being gracious toward others. It's not right to cause division over habits and practices that don't have eternal meaning. God doesn't want us to argue and fight over the insignificant details of life. He wants us to see the bigger picture. If we rise above our petty disagreements, we'll see that we are all unified by the sacrificial and undeserved love of Jesus.

Father, I don't want to put stipulations on what you allow. Transform my mindsets and give me your perspective. Help me focus on what really matters.

In Time

"What I am doing you do not understand now, but you will know after this."

JOHN 13:7 NKJV

No doubt you have heard the saying hindsight is 20/20. The meaning of this is that we can see the past clearly even when it seemed cloudy in the moment. The same thing is true about God's kingdom. We cannot always see God's hand at work, but we know that he is tying everything together with his mercy and grace.

We won't understand every chapter of our story. We won't always get the answers we want, and some things will remain a mystery until we are face-to-face with the Lord. There is a level of ignorance that must be embraced if we are going to follow Jesus. We operate by faith, and we trust that God has everything under control. Just because we can't see each piece doesn't mean we lose faith in the bigger picture.

Lord, when I struggle to understand what you are doing, help me trust that it will become clear with time. Open my eyes to see the fingerprints of your love in the details of my life. Give me faith to follow you without hesitation.

NOVEMBER 25

Plans of Promise

*"I declare the end from the beginning,
and from long ago what is not yet done,
saying: my plan will take place,
and I will do all my will."*

ISAIAH 46:10 CSB

God has not forgotten a single promise he has made, nor will any of his plans be sidetracked. God's timing is often different from ours. This can be frustrating when we cannot see any movement in areas where we long for breakthrough. God is faithful even when we have doubts. He will keep all of his promises.

Let's throw our anchor of hope into the ocean of God's mercy and kindness. Everything about him exudes steadiness and loyal love. He does not make flippant promises. He always follows through on what he says. His plans are laden with kindness, peace, and justice. They are for our good and his glory. We can count on him because he is trustworthy.

Lord, you see the end from the beginning. You have not forgotten a single promise from any generation. I believe you will fulfill them all! Strengthen my faith and give me resolve in the midst of doubt.

NOVEMBER 26

Reason to Sing

Sing for joy, O heavens!
Rejoice, O earth!
Burst into song, O mountains!
For the LORD has comforted his people
and will have compassion on them in their suffering.

ISAIAH 49:13 NLT

Do you ever wonder why there are so many love songs? Though poets and musicians have been writing songs for millennia, we still feel inspired to write new ones. Love is a topic that never grows old. We were created in love, and we were made to experience the perfection of God's love.

There is no greater reason to sing than the love of God. While we might search for love in a myriad of places, his presence is the true source. The fulfillment we find anywhere else is temporary. He is the only one who is truly worthy of our affection. The love we experience from him is pure and perfect. Nothing else can compare!

God, your love means everything to me. Without your love I would be lost. Hear my songs of gratitude and bless me with your presence. Draw me back to you whenever I wander toward lesser loves.

NOVEMBER 27

Timely Words

*A person finds joy in giving an apt reply—
and how good is a timely word!*

Proverbs 15:23 NIV

Timely words are sweet and nourishing. They are like a healing balm to an open wound. They bring comfort, strength, courage, and clarity. There are many possible effects of timely words, but they are always good for both the teller and the hearer.

When we choose to carefully consider our words with others, we grow in wisdom and discernment. We train our hearts to look for what is true, helpful, and loving. The truth doesn't need to be delivered harshly in order for it to stick. In fact, the most powerful truth is communicated with gentleness and respect.

Holy Spirit, I want to grow in wisdom and discernment. Give me self-control and help me measure my words against the truth. May everything I say reflect your character. Teach me how to be a gentle and kind communicator.

NOVEMBER 28

Incomparable Glory

> I consider that the sufferings of this present time are not worth comparing with the glory that is to be revealed to us.
>
> ROMANS 8:18 ESV

Our hardships cannot be compared to the unmatched glory to come. We are in the process of becoming more like the Lord through the hills and valleys of this life. As we submit to him, he transforms us into his likeness. We haven't experienced the fullness of his perfection, but it is promised. It is our blessed assurance.

When we need courage to persevere, let's turn to the Lord. We have an open line to the Father through Jesus. Though we cannot experience the fullness of God yet, we can receive glimpses of his glory as he reveals himself to us. As we seek his face, we will see his beauty. When we see his beauty, we will be more inspired to love, know, and serve him.

Glorious God, nothing compares to you. There is so much beauty, peace, and delight in your presence. Wash over me again and strengthen me by your gracious Spirit.

NOVEMBER 29

Courage to Wait

*Wait for the LORD's help.
Be strong and brave,
and wait for the LORD's help.*

PSALM 27:14 NCV

Some situations require action while others require patience and a steadfast heart. Waiting for God to intervene isn't easy, but it does strengthen our faith. We cannot control the outcome of every problem we face, but we don't have to. God is faithful. He will tell us when it's time to move, and when it's time to wait.

Sitting back and waiting might be hard for you. It can help to shift your perspective. Waiting is not equal to apathy. When you actively wait on God you display courage, self-control, and trust. Waiting shows that you understand God's character, and you believe he will do what he says. May God empower you to wait with courage.

God, waiting is not easy, but it is worth it when you are the one I am waiting on. When I am tempted to take control, remind me that your help is worth waiting for.

NOVEMBER 30

Perfect God

> Yahweh, what a perfect God you are!
> All Yahweh's promises have proven true.
> What a secure shelter for all those who
> turn to hide themselves in you.
>
> Psalm 18:30 tpt

When relationships are less than perfect, it's easy to transfer our disappointment to God. It takes maturity to separate God's character from the behavior of other people. Where people fall short, God is perfect. No matter how many times we are let down, his loyal love remains. When we are overlooked, betrayed, or even abused, God is our secure shelter.

God is the perfect parent, friend, and partner. He never hides motives, spins the truth, or breaks trust. His love motivates all he does, and his intentions are pure. He is the most secure shelter to hide in no matter how fierce our storms are. He hems us in with perfect love on all sides.

God, I want to know you more today. Wrap me in your love and bring healing, restoration, and hope to my heart. I trust you to be faithful and loyal even when people aren't.

December

"I will refresh the weary
and satisfy the faint."

JEREMIAH 31:25 NIV

DECEMBER 1

Wonderful News

The Spirit of the Lord God is upon me,
Because the LORD anointed me
To bring good news to the humble;
He has sent me to bind up the brokenhearted.

ISAIAH 61:1 NASB

The gospel is not simply good news; it is wonderful! God brings healing to the brokenhearted, liberation to captives, and freedom to prisoners. There is no trial or trouble that can stand against the power of his redemption. Nothing is impossible with his saving grace! He can turn even the most desolate wasteland into a lush rainforest filled with life and hope.

We have every reason to hope because of Jesus. He is our liberator, healer, teacher, and friend. He is all that we long for and so much more than we can imagine. May we know the power of his hope that lives within us today!

Lord God, you are my hope, strength, and joy. Let your good news reach every weary heart! May we all rejoice in the truth of your liberating love.

DECEMBER 2

Plans for Unity

He made known to us the mystery of his will, according to his good pleasure that he purposed in Christ as a plan for the right time—to bring everything together in Christ, both things in heaven and things on earth in him.

EPHESIANS 1:9-10 CSB

Everything is brought together in Christ. All things in heaven and earth find their center in him. Christ is the great unifier, and he does not create dissention. When we hear messages that divide or cause disunity, let's remember that Jesus isn't the cause.

Love brings us closer to one another, while fear separates us. Christ's living love is a balm for every kind of brokenness. Let's rest in the power of his mercy while extending it to others. Instead of looking for reasons to withhold love from others today, let's choose to look for reasons to offer it. There is unifying power in the love of Christ.

Jesus, bring everything together in your living love and break the power of fear in my life. I choose your way over mine. Teach me how to create unity rather than division.

DECEMBER 3

His Faithfulness

*Trust in the LORD, and do good;
Dwell in the land, and feed on His faithfulness.*

PSALM 37:3 NKJV

Following the Lord is not complicated. Scripture reminds us that God does not have an impossible list of standards for us to meet. Jesus said that as we learn more about him, we will see that he is kind, humble, and easy to please. The more we discover the faithfulness of God's character, the more we understand how incredibly simple his requirements are.

We so often complicate what God says and make our relationship with him more complicated than it needs to be. We can rest in God's faithfulness and do good to others. The loyal love of God is our bread and water; it is our refreshment and our strength. Let's feed on his faithfulness even today!

Faithful Lord, I trust you as God and Savior. Thank you for the reminder that following you is simple. I rest in your faithfulness and trust you to lead me.

DECEMBER 4

Undeniably Faithful

*If we are faithless, he remains faithful,
for he cannot disown himself.*

2 Timothy 2:13 NIV

It is incredibly powerful to know that no matter what we do, we cannot mess up the plans of God. He will do what he promised. He will fulfill his vows with the faithfulness of his own nature. He cannot turn back on his own character. His faithfulness is sure.

We can learn from God's powerful love and unshakable character. No matter what others do or choose, we can remain true to our principles. Though others may lie and cheat, we can remain faithful to our word. We cannot control how others act, but we can be responsible for our own behavior. We will never be perfect, but we can be honest, loving, humble, and gracious.

Faithful God, your loyal nature is astounding. Your unchanging ways are incredible. I want to be more like you. May my character remain unwavering no matter how other people behave.

He Keeps Track

> You keep track of all my sorrows.
> You have collected all my tears in your bottle.
> You have recorded each one in your book.
>
> PSALM 56:8 NLT

Though we may move on from our sorrows, God doesn't forget what we've gone through. He keeps track of our tears and struggles. He knows the pain we've experienced, and he holds it gently. He is familiar with our hurt even when no one else knows about it.

Not only does God see your pain and heartbreak, but he meets you in it. When others don't understand your grief, he does. Don't stay away from the Lord when you are hurt. He is your comforter, and he always knows just what you need. He will not turn away from your sadness, and he is not overwhelmed by it. God is always ready to wrap you in the warmth of his love.

God, thank you for the reassurance that I don't have to pretend with you. I can bring you my raw and vulnerable emotions, and you don't shrink back. Meet me here and minister to my heart.

DECEMBER 6

Leave It to God

I said in my heart, God will judge the righteous and the wicked, for there is a time for every matter and for every work.

ECCLESIASTES 3:17 ESV

It is not our job to push for the judgment of others' souls. Though there is a place for standing upon righteousness and promoting justice, it is never our place to assume another's intentions. God is the only wise judge who knows the heart of every person. We don't need to take his role upon ourselves.

We can trust God even when evil runs rampant in the world and corruption seems to go unchecked. There is a day coming when every heart will be weighed and measured by the Lord. He is the only one who can bear the weight of that burden. He does not take his responsibility lightly, and he is fully capable of being merciful and just at the same time. We leave judgment in the hands of God because he is the only one worthy of the job.

Lord, it can be easy to stand in judgment of others, but it is a waste of my energy. Instead, give me strength to love others without judgment. I trust you to do what only you can. Keep my heart soft and free of criticism.

DECEMBER 7

Godlike

The Son reflects the glory of God and shows exactly what God is like. He holds everything together with his powerful word.

HEBREWS 1:3 NCV

Jesus, the Son of God, revealed the nature of God to everyone. Through Jesus' ministry of compassion, teaching, and healing, he showed us what the Father is really like. We have the privilege of knowing our Maker because Jesus made a way.

Jesus healed and restored physical lives, and he cleansed people from their sins and offered them freedom of heart, mind, and soul. His entire life was focused on setting captives free and declaring God's love and mercy. What a powerfully kind and wonderful Savior he was, is, and always will be! Find your rest and hope in Christ's gracious mercy which perfectly reveals the heart of the Father.

Father, when I read the Word, may I see it through the lens of Christ who revealed your beautiful nature. Move in my heart, mind, body, and soul today. Show me more of who you are and fill me with peace as I seek you.

DECEMBER 8

Eternal Home

*Lord, you have always been our eternal home,
our hiding place from generation to generation.*

PSALM 90:1 TPT

From generation to generation, the Lord remains faithful. He does not change with shifting trends. His nature doesn't alter over time. His values of mercy, truth, peace, and joy have not diminished in the least. Though we often struggle to understand God, he is unchanging and powerfully kind to all who come to him.

God remains the one and only. He has been our eternal home, and he will continue to be. Look at previous generations and how God loved them. He was faithful to lead each person who came before us. Their stories can encourage us as we remember that God has not changed. We can count on his loyal love with every breath we take.

Lord, you are my eternal home, and I find peace in your powerful presence. Thank you for your continued faithfulness. May I be encouraged by the past and hopeful for the future.

The Seeing God

Then she called the name of the Lord who spoke to her, "You are a God who sees me"; for she said, "Have I even seen Him here and lived after He saw me?"

GENESIS 16:13 NASB

Hagar, though often portrayed as the antagonist, was only being obedient to her mistress when she slept with Abram. When she became pregnant, Sarai began to treat her badly. Hagar fled her presence and was helplessly alone. In the midst of loneliness and despair, God revealed himself to her.

It was kind of God to show up for Hagar. She was encouraged to know that God saw her and recognized her troublesome circumstances. In the same way, God sees each of us. He speaks the truth over us, and he gives us hope when we are lost in the wilderness. Though Sarai acted cruelly, God acted kindly. May we err on the side of love and understanding just as our good Father does.

God, you know exactly what I'm going through, and I need your presence. Speak to me today and encourage me as I look to you. You are the God who sees me, and I love you.

DECEMBER 10

Honest Surrender

"Father, if it is Your will, take this cup away from Me; nevertheless not My will, but Yours, be done."

LUKE 22:42 NKJV

Jesus was the Son of God. He knew what was ahead of him, and he wasn't without fear or hesitation. In his final hours he asked God if there was another way. In his humanity, he did not want to die. He did not want to experience intense pain and suffering. Does this make him any less perfect? By no means. He was fully God and fully human. He was honest with his Father in prayer, yet his final act displayed surrender and obedience.

There are some situations that loom over us and intimidate us. Not everything we are called to is easy or without pain. Sometimes the right thing is difficult. May we take the lead of Jesus and offer our honest surrender. We can have doubts and still trust God. We can share our fearful hearts and remain faithful to God's plan.

Lord Jesus, thank you for not holding back your honest prayer to the Father. When I want to give up, give me the strength I need to keep following you. I trust there is glory on the other side of my obedience.

The Better Choice

"Martha, Martha, you are worried and upset about many things, but one thing is necessary. Mary has made the right choice, and it will not be taken away from her."

Luke 10:40-42 CSB

There will always be more to accomplish. Martha was overwhelmed by her tasks, and she prioritized them over connecting with Jesus. When we are worried and upset about many things, it is hard to choose to rest. Though it feels counterproductive, resting is exactly what Jesus invites us to do.

Martha represents a common struggle we face. Most of us find it difficult to lay down our worries and rest at the feet of Jesus. Let's remember that God will never condemn us for choosing to sit in his presence and listen to his wisdom. Our to-do lists can wait. It is better to be found at his feet than to be overcome by the demands of life.

Lord, I choose to spend time with you and rest in your presence. Give me grace to lay aside the endless tasks I have in front of me. They won't change, but time with you will change my heart.

DECEMBER 12

God's Home

> I heard a loud shout from the throne, saying, "Look, God's home is now among his people! He will live with them, and they will be his people. God himself will be with them."
>
> REVELATION 21:3 NLT

One day, we will have more than a spiritual home in Christ's kingdom. We will find our forever home with God, and nothing will separate us from his glory. We will physically see him face to face for all eternity. He will be our sun and shield, bringing light to all.

It is impossible to imagine the full glory of God's presence. It is more beautiful than anything we've seen. What a glorious reality awaits us in the fullness of his kingdom! It is worth all that we sacrifice and so much more. May we rely on his peace, wisdom, and love to guide us into greater goodness until we stand face to face with God Almighty.

God, I can't wait to see you in the fullness of your glory. May my heart stay ready in love to embrace all that you lead me in. I trust you, and I love you!

DECEMBER 13

Our High Priest

Because Jesus lives forever, he has a permanent priesthood. Therefore he is able to save completely those who come to God through him, because he always lives to intercede for them.

HEBREWS 7:24-25 NIV

Jesus' work didn't end on the cross. After everything he went through on our behalf, he still sits at the right hand of the Father interceding for us. He is our great advocate, and he always will be. What a wonder to know that he not only saves us, but he continues to support us.

There is no one greater than Jesus Christ to bring our case before the Father. He has done all that is necessary to create a bridge to the Father's presence. He is the way, the truth, and the life. He is the door to the Father, and we enter through him. He is our great confidence, and his love and grace cover us fully. As we surrender to him, his righteousness becomes our own. What a powerful gift!

High Priest, I bring you everything that is on my heart and mind, and I know you will relieve my fears. I find clarity, peace, and joy in your presence. Thank you for being my Savior and my advocate.

DECEMBER 14

Even to the End

"I am with you always, to the end of the age."
MATTHEW 28:20 ESV

Jesus' presence is with us through the fellowship of the Holy Spirit. We are never alone because Jesus knew we would need a constant companion. He has offered us everything we need to remain faithful until he returns. The Holy Spirit is our greatest teacher, encourager, and friend. He is a gift more valuable than anything we can find in this world.

The Holy Spirit is Jesus' promise to you. Don't leave your gift unopened and unused. Lean into the presence of the one who never leaves you or forsakes you. Take full advantage of his willingness to help you and encourage you. You are never alone, and you have access to all of God's wisdom no matter what is going on in your life.

Jesus, thank you for the gift of the Holy Spirit. Teach me how to rely on him as I walk through life. Thank you for your faithful help and encouragement.

DECEMBER 15

Foundations of Love

I pray that Christ will live in your hearts by faith and that your life will be strong in love and be built on love.

EPHESIANS 3:17 NCV

Faith, hope, and love are the eternal virtues of God's kingdom. The greatest of these is love. When we build our lives on the solid foundation of God's love, we will not be shaken. God's love is reliable, steady, and unchanging. The law of God's love is the very foundation of his kingdom.

When we put our faith in Christ's living love, we will grow strong in mercy and kindness. As we follow his example, love will exude from our lives. Living according to God's law of love is our best option. A foundation of love keeps us safe and secure no matter what is going on in the world. Even when everything around us is shaking, love remains.

Lord, when it all fades away, your love remains. Help me prioritize love above everything else in my life. May my words and actions display your love to the people around me.

DECEMBER 16

Flawless Before Him

> Our faith in Jesus transfers God's righteousness to us and he now declares us flawless in his eyes. This means we can now enjoy true and lasting peace with God, all because of what our Lord Jesus, the Anointed One, has done for us.
>
> ROMANS 5:1 TPT

Peace is not found by relying on the ways of the world. True peace can only be found in Christ. He is our righteousness and saving grace. The peace he offers is permanent and cannot be taken away from us. He gives us courage and strength that doesn't depend on the shifting sands of the world.

In faith, we believe that Jesus is the Son of God and the Savior of the world. He broke the chains of sin and death and removed our guilt and shame. His righteousness has become our righteousness, and we stand flawlessly before him. Let's rest in the confidence of his peace as we live in the light of his great love.

Righteous One, thank you for doing what no one else could by removing all barriers between God and mankind. My faith is in you, and you have become my righteousness. I am yours. Let your peace reign in my heart.

DECEMBER 17

Gracious God

You, Lord, are a compassionate and gracious God,
Slow to anger and abundant in mercy and truth.

PSALM 86:15 NASB

No matter what circumstances we face, the nature of God is sure. When our hearts are troubled by the things we see in the world, we can actively turn our attention to God's unchanging character. As we do, we will find footing for our faith and peace to settle our hearts.

God is gracious, compassionate, and kind. He is not quick to judge, and he is slow to anger. He is not lacking in love, and he is abundant in mercy and truth. His powerful presence sustains us, and that power cannot be diminished by the intimidation of the world. God's ways are higher, truer, and better than the ways of this world, and he will never fail.

God, I turn my attention to your unfailing goodness. You are not vengeful or easily frustrated. You are slow to anger and abundant in compassion and mercy. What grace I find in you every time I approach your throne!

DECEMBER 18

Complete in Him

> In Him dwells all the fullness of the Godhead bodily; and you are complete in Him, who is the head of all principality and power.
>
> COLOSSIANS 2:9-10 NKJV

Jesus is the complete fullness of God in human form. This God who reigns over every kingdom and authority is our King. We are made complete in him. Jesus is the fullness of all God's goodness, and he overflows in love to everyone who opens their hearts to him.

Why would we look for wholeness from things that will never satisfy? Jesus is the fullness of all we long and hope for. Anything else that steals our attention is less worthy of our affection. He fulfills our hearts in a way nothing else can. His presence is where our souls are truly satisfied. Let's find our rest in him and receive the abundant goodness that he alone offers.

Jesus Christ, thank you for the fullness of love I find in you. Wash over me in a fresh way and give me grace to follow you alone. Draw my heart toward you and keep my gaze upon you.

DECEMBER 19

One True God

> We know that the Son of God has come and has given us understanding so that we may know the true one. We are in the true one—that is, in his Son, Jesus Christ. He is the true God and eternal life.
>
> 1 John 5:20 csb

God is love, and we know we belong to him when love defines our lives as well. We accept his love and offer it freely to everyone we come across. We experience great grace and mercy, and we generously do the same for others without discrimination. This is the way of God's kingdom.

Jesus is with you every step of the way. He readily helps you as you endeavor to love people as he did. He equips you, and he encourages you as you do your best to share God's love. He gives you abundant freedom, peace, joy, love, and patience. As you walk along his path, he does not leave you empty handed.

Savior, you are worth my worship and devotion. Thank you for equipping me to love others well. Fill my life with good fruit as I follow you. Thank you for the abundant gifts I find in your presence.

DECEMBER 20

So Close

*The LORD is close to all who call on him,
yes, to all who call on him in truth.*

PSALM 145:18 NLT

Today's verse is a promise you can count on. You can be confident that God is with you. When you call on him from a heart that is true, God is close. If you are in Christ, let every doubt fall away as you call out to him. He is your promised peace, and his presence is not far away.

There is assurance in the closeness of God's love as it washes over us. We don't have to worry about whether God hears us or not. He listens to all who call out to him, and he answers. There is power in persistence, for we will receive the answers we long for. There is also peace in the confidence of God's faithfulness. Let's move this faith from our heads to our hearts and receive the power of his peace.

Lord, I am desperate for the lived knowledge of your nearness. Show me just how close you are to me today. Thank you for being faithful at all times.

DECEMBER 21

Confident Help

We say with confidence, "The Lord is my helper; I will not be afraid. What can mere mortals do to me?"

HEBREWS 13:6 NIV

The threats of others may make our hearts quake for a moment, but God is our confident help. He is the defender of the weak. He helps and delivers those who call out to him. Furthermore, he sanctifies our souls and gives us eternal safety. Though our flesh may fail, our hearts and souls thrive in God's present peace.

When we don't feel confident, we can turn to the Lord for help. The more we experience his faithfulness, the surer we become of his goodness. God's nature is unfailing, and he won't leave us without the power of his great love in our hearts. Let's put our trust in him no matter how we feel today. He is faithful regardless.

Lord, you are my help and strength. You give me courage in the face of fear, and I trust you with my life.

DECEMBER 22

Glorious Gift

The Word became flesh and dwelt among us, and we have seen his glory, glory as of the only Son from the Father, full of grace and truth.

JOHN 1:14 ESV

Jesus' birth, life, death, and resurrection reveal the glory of God. Jesus embraced humanity so that we would know God. He chose to humble himself in order to reveal the glory and unstoppable love of the Father. He left the perfection of heaven to share it with us.

As we study the life of Christ, we learn about the character of God. Through Jesus we can understand how God moves on the earth. We can have reasonable expectations of who God is and how he interacts with us. Furthermore, we have fellowship with the Holy Spirit. He guides us with his presence and points us toward truth. He opens the eyes and ears of our hearts that we may understand the power of God in our own lives.

Jesus, speak to me today. Please give me a deeper understanding of your truth. Thank you for the power of your life and the gift of the Holy Spirit.

DECEMBER 23

God With Us

The Lord himself will give you a sign: The virgin will conceive and give birth to a son, and will call him Immanuel.

ISAIAH 7:14 NIV

The Messiah was promised for generations before he was born to Mary. The long-awaited king did not come in royal robes and with proclamations of glory. He chose to be humble and lowly. Rather than orchestrating an extravagant entrance, he was born to a teenager in a stable among animals.

God chose simple circumstances to reveal the glory of his love through Jesus. Jesus lacked no good thing even though his family was humble. Let's not despise our own humble beginnings or our less than extraordinary lives. God meets us in the mundane. He touches the ordinary things in our lives and makes them supernatural. There is grace, peace, and hope in the power of God's presence no matter how basic our circumstances seem.

Immanuel, thank you for choosing to show God's glory through humble circumstances. I trust you will do that in my own life. Your presence is all that matters.

DECEMBER 24

Making the Best of It

When they arrived in Bethlehem, Mary went into labor, and there she gave birth to her firstborn son. She wrapped the newborn baby in strips of cloth, and Mary and Joseph laid him in a feeding trough since there was no available space in any upper room in the village.

Luke 2:6-7 TPT

It wasn't the best of circumstances when Mary went into labor without a place to stay. Anyone who has given birth knows exactly how stressful and disappointing that would be. Jesus was born in a barn and placed in a trough. His birth was as humble as it could have been.

Despite their circumstances, Mary and Joseph made the most of what they'd been given. We can follow their example when faced with our own humble circumstances. When things are less than ideal, let's remember that there is room for Jesus. We can offer him what we have, and he will graciously accept it. We can welcome him into our disorderly spaces, and he will not scorn us.

Jesus, I welcome you into my life even when it feels like a mess. I trust you will make yourself at home. Bless me with your presence and fill my heart with your love.

DECEMBER 25

Wonderful Counselor

A Child will be born to us, a Son will be given to us;
And the government will rest on His shoulders;
And His name will be called Wonderful Counselor,
Mighty God, Eternal Father, Prince of Peace.

ISAIAH 9:6 NASB

Jesus' arrival was prophesied long before it happened. His titles were spoken into existence before he ever bore them. Those who waited for him had clear expectations of who he would be. They anxiously awaited a counselor, king, and father. Though he is all those things and more, Jesus was so humble that many missed him altogether.

Our expectations are not foolproof. We cannot perfectly imagine the details of the unknown. Let's hold our expectations loosely so we don't miss the goodness that's right in front of us. There are beautiful gifts of grace available through Christ if we have eyes to see. Though he wasn't what the people expected, Christ's saving grace is more glorious than could have been imagined.

Jesus, though you arrived in a different package than many expected, you were beautiful in all your ways. Give me grace to adjust my expectations when needed. I don't want to miss the gifts you give because I am waiting for something different.

DECEMBER 26

Great Mystery

*Without controversy great is the mystery of godliness:
God was manifested in the flesh,
Justified in the Spirit,
Seen by angels,
Preached among the Gentiles,
Believed on in the world,
Received up in glory.*

1 TIMOTHY 3:16 NKJV

Godliness has been revealed to us through the life of Jesus. He is our righteousness. Yielding our lives to his leadership and receiving the power of his resurrection life is the only way for us to be with God. We cannot achieve goodliness by our own resolve. Christ alone is our means.

Let's lift our eyes above the fray of this world. There are many distractions to keep us from looking up to the one who reigns in glory. Our great High Priest sits at the right hand of the Father making intercession for us. He intervenes on our behalf. We are justified before God because Jesus advocates for us.

Lord Jesus, you are worthy of my trust and surrender. You are my only means for godliness. Thank you for intervening in my life and calling me your own.

His Promise

"I will not leave you as orphans; I am coming to you."

JOHN 14:18 CSB

Jesus did not leave us without hope. He promised that his followers would not be left alone. We cannot walk with him in the flesh, but he is with us by the Spirit. He has given us a companion who consistently reminds us of the truth. The Holy Spirit reveals Jesus to all who are looking for him.

Jesus meets us through the power of the Holy Spirit. We are never alone. God is with us no matter what we face. He is our faithful help, but we must rely on him. He is trustworthy and true, and everything he does is good and right. He blesses us with presence now, and he will come back again to make all things right.

Lord, I hold on to your promises, and I ask for your powerful presence to meet me today. Thank you for the peace, joy, and hope I always find in you.

DECEMBER 28

Listen to Jesus

Jesus overheard them and said to Jairus, "Don't be afraid. Just have faith."

MARK 5:36 NLT

Jairus went to Jesus to ask him to heal his daughter. Before he even got the chance, word arrived that his daughter had died. This is where today's verse begins. Jesus overheard the news and spoke hope to Jairus. He went with Jairus to his home, and there he brought the girl back to life!

You can imagine the doubt that was present on that day. The crowd laughed in response to Jesus saying that the little girl was just asleep. When Jesus tells us to have faith in the midst of fear, let's take his word for it. His powerful presence goes with us and brings life where there is devastation. Despite the harsh realities of this world, there is always hope.

Lord, help me hear your voice above the crowd. I want to know what you say. Speak into the specific challenges I face. You have what I need.

DECEMBER 29

Established by God

> In their hearts humans plan their course,
> but the Lord establishes their steps.
>
> PROVERBS 16:9 NIV

Today's verse is not an indictment against making plans. It is natural and necessary to chart our course to the best of our ability. At the same time, we cannot foresee all the challenges that will come our way. We don't need to worry even when the unexpected happens. Jesus establishes our steps, and he's never caught off-guard.

When our plans go off course, let's not become discouraged. It may surprise us, but it doesn't surprise God. He is able to lead us through the twists and turns of this life with confident kindness. There is nothing we need to fret about when we trust the Lord to guide our steps. He is good, and he will never fail.

God, though I make my plans, I hold them loosely before you. I trust you to guide me into your goodness. When darkness falls, I hold tighter to your hand and listen for your voice.

DECEMBER 30

Eagerly Waiting

Through the Spirit, by faith, we ourselves eagerly wait for the hope of righteousness.

GALATIANS 5:5 ESV

It's important to be aware of what holds our attention. We will wander toward whatever we are gazing at. If we are focused on the past, we won't experience the goodness of the present. If our eyes are on our troubles, we will be filled with despair rather than hope.

When we shift our perspective toward the hope of righteousness, it can energize our footsteps and give us endurance. Our focus should be on God as we eagerly wait for him to fulfill his promises. With our eyes on him, we will not wander from the path he has marked out for us. We go from glory to glory until we stand in his presence.

Lord, you have my attention. Keep my eyes firmly on you as I wait for the hope of righteousness. You are the way, the truth, and the life. I trust you to lead me for all my days.

DECEMBER 31

Radiating Goodness

"For you who honor me, goodness will shine on you like the sun, with healing in its rays. You will jump around, like well-fed calves."

MALACHI 4:2 NCV

As we look ahead, let's take this Scripture to heart. Goodness, healing, and life-giving love have been promised to us. There is more beauty, grace, peace, love, and joy to experience ahead. Wherever this year takes us, let us honor the Lord and stand unabashedly soaking in the goodness of his grace.

As we stand on the precipice of a new year, let's not forget to spend time in the presence of our powerful King. Let's honor what he has done in and through us over the last year. Let's remember his goodness and faithfulness. He did not forsake you over the past year, and he will be with you for the next. The best is yet to come!

Lord, you are the sun, and I stand before you. Thank you for all you've done, all you are doing, and all you have yet to do. You are kind, good, and faithful. Remind me of your goodness and help me hold fast to your promises.